Stalking
the
Good Life

Also by Euell Gibbons:

Stalking the Wild Asparagus
Stalking the Blue-Eyed Scallop
Stalking the Healthful Herbs
The Beachcomber's Handbook
Feast on a Diabetic Diet

This book is printed on recycled paper.

Stalking
the
Good Life

My Love Affair with Nature

by EUELL GIBBONS

illustrated by
FREDA GIBBONS

DAVID McKAY COMPANY, INC.
New York

STALKING THE GOOD LIFE

Fourth Printing, June 1971

Library of Congress Catalog Card Number: 77-146480

MANUFACTURED IN THE UNITED STATES OF AMERICA

VAN REES PRESS · NEW YORK

This book is dedicated to the lively, joyous, and joy-giving group of teenagers who are the enthusiastic members of the ecology class in Germantown Friends School in Philadelphia, and to their teacher, John Boles, competent naturalist, discerning ecologist, inspired educator, and a great human being.

I am deeply grateful to the editors of *Organic Gardening and Farming Magazine* for permission to use the material published in their magazine. I am also indebted to all primitive peoples past and present who have accumulated the knowledge that I have used.

Contents

Foraging
for
Survival

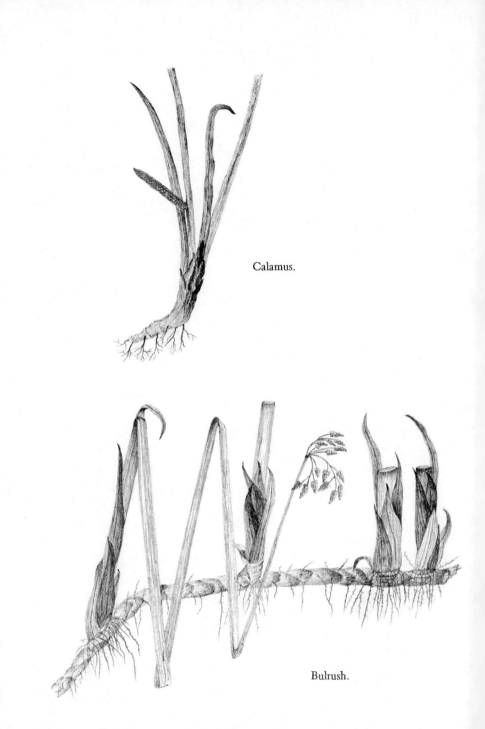

Calamus.

Bulrush.

1. Wilderness Survival

NOT long ago, I came upon a great and true story in a magazine concerning a couple who had themselves marooned on an uninhabited island in Lake Superior with a few pieces of essential equipment, and no food whatsoever, to live for two weeks on what they could wrest from nature.

The couple were not unprepared for such an experience. The husband had considerable wilderness experience and was a hunter and fisherman. They carried a gun and ammunition, fishline and hooks, and planned to live mostly on game and fish. However, game seemed to be largely nonexistent, and they had difficulty finding anything with which to bait their fishhooks. When they finally shot a squirrel and used his meat for bait, either there were no fish in the vicinity or those that were did not fancy squirrel.

The marooned wanderers ate blueberries, reindeer moss, waterlily tubers, violet leaves, and the one kind of mushroom out of many growing on the island that they knew to be safe. They finally killed a single grouse and caught a few fish. They survived, and except for losing some weight, came off the island in pretty good shape.

I admire this pair; they had taken along a sealed emergency kit containing food, sleeping bags, stove and fuel, medical supplies, and signal flares. But according to the rules they had agreed to follow, they were not to open this kit unless they decided to abandon the experiment. They stuck it out, and the emergency kit was still sealed at the end of two weeks. Their adventure makes exciting reading.

In following this tale, I discovered why my own survival experiences don't seem to make for truly adventurous stories. Every writer knows that a good story must have elements of struggle and conflict with obstacles to be overcome, as did this one. But since I approach nature with a spirit of cooperation rather than conflict, there isn't much struggle to liven up things. The element of suspense is missing, since the outcome is never in doubt. There I am, lying around out in the woods, stuffing myself with so many kinds of wild foods that I invariably grow fat. I hesitate to compare my own easy survival trips with the great experience of this couple, for several reasons. For one thing, they existed solely on wild food for two weeks, while the longest I have ever sustained entirely on wild food is six days. For another thing, they chose an area where wild foods are pretty hard to come by, while I usually pick some site where I suspect that wild food will be plentiful.

When I go on my survival trips, I look first for some abundant source of plant food that can keep my belly filled and my energy up, and only after that do I start looking for fish, or other animal foods, to balance my diet and make it more palatable.

I did go on one survival trip last summer in country just about as poor as that in which the Snooks had their adventure. This was in the Quetiquo Provincial Park, a huge wilderness area in southern Ontario, not very far—as the loon flies—from where the Snooks had their camp, and very much the same kind of country. I was teaching wilderness survival to the students of Outward Bound School in northern Minnesota at the time.

The students were having survival tests while on an expedition up in Quetiquo, and they came back complaining that they could not find the edible plants I had taught them to recognize up in that area. Even the instructors said that edible plants were almost nonexistent there. It became obvious that I must go up and explore the actual territory where the survival tests were held if I were to teach successfully. For the first time I was going on a survival trip into an area not because wild foods were reported to be lush and abundant, but because they were reported to be very meager.

Since I could be away from the school only a few days, I decided to go by plane. A medical student who manned our first-aid station agreed to accompany me. Planes are not allowed to land in Quetiquo, so our chartered craft took us and our canoe to a lake just outside the park boundary, which was connected to another lake inside the park by a ten-mile-long narrow, winding stream just barely navigable by canoe.

All we were trying to prove was that there was enough wild food in this area to survive, so we didn't try to stint ourselves on other comforts. We had sleeping bags and a mosquito-proof tent. We carried hunting knives on our belts, and I had a fishing rod and a few lures. Since we wanted to approximate the eating conditions endured by the students on their survival tests, we did not carry cooking utensils, and our only food supply was a package of salt, which was allowed students.

We did not carry guns. If we had, and had we wanted to disobey several game laws, we could have had a thousand pounds of good red meat in the first few hours. As we paddled down that narrow creek and around a sharp bend, we came on a great bull moose with his head under water feeding on bottom plants. We glided up to within five feet of him, and when he lifted his huge, antlered head from the water, I found myself eyeball to eyeball with half a ton of wild beast. I'll never forget the look in those great brown eyes. It was compounded of confusion, stupidity, and a suffering, hurt look. For a minute we stared at one another, almost within touching distance. Gradually I could see intelligence and caution dawn in those big eyes, and finally he must have realized that we could be dangerous, for he whirled about, splashing us with water, and lumbered up the bank and off into the woods.

It was a bad time of year. The wild strawberries were all gone, and the blueberries hadn't begun to ripen. On our journey upstream we ate some bluebead-lily leaves, which were plentiful, and at one place found a few dozen dwarf raspberries (*Rubus pubescens*), which we gobbled. This is a delicious fruit, but unfortunately each plant bears only a single berry. We found a patch of calamus (*Acorus calamus*) growing in the water and stopped for lunch. I was delighted to find that this northern calamus has a large and tender heart with a milder flavor than the calamus native to Pennsylvania. Still, any calamus is very spicy and more of a flavoring than a staple, so we soon tired of that gingery bite. We gathered some for future reference, and went on, still half hungry.

When we reached the lake where we intended to camp, the sun was already lowering. My companion wanted fish for dinner, so I started casting as he paddled slowly about the lake. The fish just weren't biting. I wasn't too worried, because all around the lake in the shallows were great fields of bulrushes. When my casting arm grew tired, and I did, too, from the hours of paddling, I suggested we have a bulrush dinner. We pulled our canoe into one of the bulrush patches and started eating. When a great American bulrush is pulled, it usually breaks just where it is joined onto the parent rhizome. Peel the base and one discovers a tender, white, cylindrical heart about three inches long and half an inch through. This has a slightly sweet flavor and is crisp, mild, and very pleasant to eat. They are easily found, and their mild flavor keeps you from growing tired of them, so we stuffed ourselves. As the free sugar in them leaped directly into our blood streams, we could feel our energy returning even as we ate.

It was getting late and time to camp. Someone had cleared a

path through the bulrushes to a fine campsite. As soon as we went ashore I felt thankful that one previous camper had been a litterbug, for he had left behind a gallon can that formerly contained fuel for a camp stove. By cutting off the top, I had a cooking pot.

While my buddy set up camp, I went down to the shore and began casting along that long canoe path through the bulrushes. After a few casts I felt something hit the lure—and soon had an eight-pound great northern pike on shore. Here was food indeed! I skinned and filleted this big fish, and since northerns are mostly head, I got two fillets that weighed about a pound and a half apiece. I stuck green sticks on either side of the fire and wove switches between them, then pinned the fillets to this rack and broiled them. We actually finished every morsel of those huge chunks of fish. I put the meaty bones and skin and head of the fish into the cooking pot and boiled them for next day's *bouillabaisse*. With stomachs tight and comfortable, we hit the sack.

I was up before the sun, looking for more food. While peeling bulrushes, I noticed wild mint at the water's edge and gathered some to make the morning's tea. Behind a jutting peninsula I found a thick patch of cattails, some still young enough to have tender hearts. This "Cossack asparagus," as it is sometimes called, is a delicious, nutritious vegetable. On the running end of each rhizome is a snow-white, horn-shaped sprout that will be next year's cattails. These sprouts make an even better vegetable than the hearts. Each rhizome also has a core of almost pure starch, which is very good cooked. I carried these treasures back to camp for breakfast. We had fragrant cups of mint tea, brewed in a beer can someone had abandoned, and cattail sprouts and hearts, along with bulrush hearts, boiled right in that fish broth in our big cooking can.

After breakfast we went exploring on the ridge behind the camp. We found a few more dwarf raspberries, ornaments to our diet, but not enough to stave off starvation. There were tender leaves of sour sorrel (*Rumex acetosella*) whose lemon-like flavor made them pleasant for nibbles. On top of the ridge we found a great many teaberries (*Gaultheria procumbens*), sweet and with a sprightly wintergreen flavor, but I suspect that they have little food value.

Back at the camp we spent an hour pulling up sedge stalks, peeling the bases, and extracting the tiny edible part from each one. This is a starch heart, only a little more than an eighth of an inch in diameter, about three inches long, and good either raw or cooked. We picked the fishbones out of the stew, then added the sedge hearts, some cattail hearts and sliced-up cattail sprouts. For the rest of our stay there we never let that stew run out. We boiled it again every few hours to sterilize it against spoiling. Each time we heated it and ate another cupful we looked around for something else we could throw into the pot. It changed flavor every time we added ingredients. The taste ranged from awful through passable to almost good, but it was always hot, nourishing food that ironed the wrinkles out of our bellies.

To supplement the stew we ate cattail rhizomes, cut into six-inch pieces and roasted before the fire. When the outsides were browned, we peeled them and ate the inside. They tasted remotely like roast sweet potato, but were full of fiber. After chewing all the nourishment out of the fiber, we would spit it into the fire. Inelegant, but sustaining.

That afternoon we paddled over to one of the portage trails that led from our lake. Along this trail we found a dead birch covered with oyster mushrooms. There must have been fifteen pounds of these fine mushrooms on that one tree, and we took them all. The mushrooms were a delicious addition to the stew, and we also ate them broiled over the fire and salted. Near the trail we also discovered a mudhole full of small but edible leopard frogs, and that evening we had a sumptuous dinner of more broiled frogs than we could eat, with plenty left over to add to the stew.

I caught a two-pound walleye next day. That and the northern were the only two fish we caught on the entire trip. The walleye gave us another feed of broiled fish, with some left for the eternal stew. We had fallen into the habit of eating about five times a day, besides nibbling on bulrush and sedge hearts in between. We had no stomach cramps, no headaches, and were never really hungry. We could have prolonged this survival exercise, but what more could we prove? It was obvious that we could spend the rest of the summer on this lake and never lose a pound.

We added mushrooms and more water to the stew the following day, boiled it awhile, then loaded it and all our gear into the canoe for the long upstream paddle back to the lake where the airplane was to meet us. We still had a reserve of stew, cattail rhizomes, and bulrush hearts that we had to discard when we saw the plane coming in. I won't say that we didn't look forward to some civilized food—especially to steaming cups of hot coffee, but we hadn't suffered.

2. The Organic Camper

CAMPING is one of the fastest-growing sports in this country. Each summer thousands of families fill all available campsites in the national and state parks, while private camp grounds do a flourishing business on the overflow. Suppliers offer a luxurious and tempting array of camping equipment, and catering to the needs of this army of new campers has become a multimillion-dollar business. If you are willing to spend a king's ransom on beautiful commercial items, you can camp as luxuriously as you can live at a resort hotel. A really modern camper can have so many of the conveniences that he enjoys at home that he often begins to wonder why he left in the first place.

Despite its growing popularity, camping—just camping—is a very unsatisfactory recreation. One encounters campers, even in remote camps at the edge of alluring wildernesses, who know nothing about nature and couldn't care less whether or not they ever learn anything. These families are often very enthusiastic campers—for about two hours. By then the fancy equipment has been set up and sufficiently admired and the youngsters start the eternal complaint, "There's nothing to do." They are chauffeured around the surrounding towns in search of commercial swimming pools, tennis courts, soft-drink machines, hamburger stands, and spectator recreation.

Why go camping to indulge in exactly the same things that can be enjoyed at home with more ease and convenience?

Camping should not be considered an end in itself. Activities that mix best with camping are those that bring you into a closer, more intimate, relationship with nature. Besides the obvious recreations of hunting and fishing, these include such fascinating hobbies as hiking, mountain climbing, bird-watching, beachcombing, and botanizing—that is, studying and collecting plants on field trips.

Perhaps the most successful camper is the person who has already developed attitudes that enable him to wring the maximum amount of joy from the experience. He has discovered that nature must be approached in a spirit of cooperation and love. Having a deep reverence for life and for the soil from which it springs, he is the finest of conservationists, seeing to it that land and life do not suffer because he came that way.

When one has learned the techniques of living with nature, it is no longer necessary to camp in public camp grounds with all the facilities of home. One can often secure permission to camp in areas where no one else has ever set up a tent. There is a sense of fresh cleanliness about an area that has not experienced the presence of hundreds of preceding campers. Public bathhouses are a poor substitute for a clean, cold stream, and the use of a slit trench for a latrine and broad-leaved aster leaves for toilet paper does not pollute the environment nearly as much as a flush toilet that eventually drains into our waterways.

When I tell people that I prefer to camp away from the commercial and public campgrounds, they are usually quick to point out that one can't just stop and pitch a tent beside the highway or on some wayside farm. Farmers don't take kindly to such trespassers. This is generally true, of course, but I have found a great many farmers friendly and cooperative when approached in the right spirit.

You must develop skills in finding these perfect and formerly unused campgrounds. One way to do it is to get off the beaten track. Study the map and find a small road that leads off the one you are following, then a smaller road that leads off of it, and finally a still smaller road trailing off that. On this last little road one is almost certain to find an ideal camping spot where permission is either not required or easily obtained.

One reason I like to keep my camping equipment simple is because light, easily transported gear gives me more flexibility in selecting campsites. The essentials are a comfortable camp bed, good food, and protection from inclement weather and biting insects. All these can be kept light enough so you can carry them on your back, in a canoe, or in the trunk of the family car.

You'll be surprised at how few things you actually need. When my son and I took a seven-day canoe trip on the Susquehanna River I thought I had cut equipment to the bone, but still found we never used over half the things I carried along. Our campsites were always islands in the middle of the river, and permission to use them was apparently not necessary; frankly, we never inquired. I am usually a knowledge hound, but there are some things I don't want to know.

We carried a very light two-man tent, and we always pitched it, in case a rainstorm should come up at night. But during clear weather we always slept outdoors under the stars, anyway. The shores of this river are usually badly infested with mosquitoes, but strangely, the mid-river islands seem entirely clear of these obnoxious insects. Maybe the wind blows them ashore. Our beds were warm sleeping bags on air mattresses, and they were luxurious. We carried a fairly large assortment of cooking utensils, but never used any except a frying pan, a stew kettle, and a coffee pot. Meals were cooked over driftwood campfires built on river beaches where they would not endanger the woods. We took pride in leaving the islands so that no one could tell we had camped there.

We had a ball. One day we pushed the canoe into a side

stream until the water became too shallow to float it, then waded upstream seining crayfish with a minnow net. Usually thought of as fish bait, these little crustaceans are actually very good food themselves, much more delicate and delicious than shrimp, crab, or lobster. On the banks of this stream we found wild black raspberries growing in great abundance and just in the prime of ripeness. We feasted that day on crayfish tails rolled in pancake flour and fried, plus huge bowls of luscious black raspberries.

Our seining netted a few molting crayfish with soft shells. These were saved and that evening we baited hooks with them and caught a nice mess of big-mouthed bass. We also caught catfish, small sunnies, and great, huge carp on this trip. What's more, they all went into the frying pan within minutes of being caught. If it didn't happen to be mealtime when the fish were caught, so what? Paddling a canoe in that fresh air always generated enough appetite to dispose of a bite or two, and I have found that fish lifted directly from the water into the frying pan are at least ten times as good as those saved until the next day before they are cooked.

We always gathered fresh wild plants to cook as vegetables, and enjoyed cattail hearts and sprouts, poke greens and lamb's quarters on several occasions. We made tasty teas of sassafras roots, wintergreen leaves, and wild mints found growing along the river shores or on the islands. I remember a piquant, mouth-watering salad made of wild watercress and the acid leaves of sheep sorrel. We made no attempt to forage all our food, but bought whatever we wanted at riverside stores along the way.

Never did we feel the need of entertainment other than that furnished by the constantly changing panorama of the river, its shores, and its islands. Once we came upon a weird island that had been cleared of timber except for a few large trees standing dead and ghostly looking. In the midst of this grove was a huge abandoned mansion with black holes for windows and shutters hanging askew, as spooky a place as I ever saw. We decided one thing was missing, so we found a board among the driftwood on the beach and using a can of lacquer carried for canoe repairs, we painted a sign saying "BEWARE OF THE THING" and stuck it up on the shore where it could be seen by passing boat-men. Then we paddled on until we found a more cheerful island on which to pitch our tent.

Both my son and I look back on that seven-day trip as one of the most pleasant experiences we ever had. He has often ex-pressed a desire to repeat the performance, but I believe it is usually better to seek out new experiences rather than try to recapture old ones. Incidentally, I left home with only twenty dollars in my wallet and at the end of the trip I still had more than ten of it left. How cheap a vacation do you want?

We did repeat the trip after a fashion not so long ago. We loaded the canoe on top of the car and then drove along the banks of the river. At night we would load the light camping gear into the canoe, paddle out to one of the islands, and camp for the night, leaving the locked car parked on the opposite shore. Tiring of the river, we headed for the mountains. I am no great hiker, but we found that many of the camping spots along the Appalachian Trail are only a mile or less from the road. This kind of hike I can take. Parking the car, we'd load the bare essentials for camping on our backs and pack in. A tent was unnecessary here, as these campsites have Adirondack shelters with built-in bunks, and there is no charge for using them.

This simple, casual kind of camping, often on virgin sites, seems possible in every area. I have enjoyed it in most of our crowded Eastern states as well as in the Midwest, and in Texas, New Mexico, Arizona, Colorado, Utah, and Nevada, and on the West Coast from Southern California to British Columbia. It takes more time, work, and skill than merely pulling into a pub-lic or commercial campground, but the rewards are worth it.

I am often asked if one can do this kind of camping with children. This amuses me. Not only do I think children can be tolerated in a wilderness camp, I think they are essential. My greatest joy is opening young minds to the possibilities of nature and teaching them their relatedness to all forms of life.

Since my own children have grown up, I still take children on camping trips—even if I have to borrow them from the neighbors. I like to see their round eyes and round mouths and listen to the little *Oh!* of wonder that escapes them when they make a new discovery in nature, catch a fish or a frog, or merely look up at the stars where no artificial lights dim their luster. There should be such an "oh" in camping if it is to be enjoyed to the utmost!

One of my most precious camping memories is of a week spent on an island off the coast of Maine. It was not only uninhabited, but, beyond some shell mounds that indicated Indians had at least camped here, it showed no sign of previous habitation. A boatman landed my wife and me, along with two neighbor children, a boy nine and his sister eleven, and our gear, then went away, promising to return at the end of a week. We spent the afternoon setting up a comfortable camp, making our sanitary arrangements, and preparing a good supper over a driftwood campfire.

We started relating more intimately with the environment soon after supper. There was an extremely low tide shortly after dark, so we took lanterns and flashlights and went exploring tide pools, finding all sorts of strange and beautiful life forms that one never sees in the daytime. The boy, Mark, soon spotted a huge Jonah crab (*Cancer borealis*), and the expedition turned into a crab hunt, with squeals and laughs aplenty to make it a memorable occasion. There was just enough danger of being nipped by the sluggish Jonahs to give zest to the sport, and shortly we had enough crabs to furnish a glorious lunch the next day. (While camping, I prefer to search out and eat what I wouldn't find at home. I believe one's food habits and prejudices should be given a vacation, as well as one's mind and body.)

Next morning at low tide we went over the same area again, marveling at its difference when seen by daylight. We found great beds of blue mussels (*Mytilis edulis*) and on one sandy shoal an abundance of soft clam (*Mya arenaria*), both excellent seafoods that promised delicious meals. On the upper beach

Beach Pea.

grew wild roses (*Rosa rugosa*) with huge ripe rose hips as large
as good-sized plums. Inland, we discovered a great patch of wild
red raspberries (*Rubus strigosus*), heavy with ripe fruit. We split
each rose hip in half, raked out the seeds, then filled the cavities
with one luscious, ripe red raspberry to each rose hip half, making a delicious dessert that was loaded with healthful nutrition.
On another part of the island shore we found a large patch of
beach peas (*Lathyrus maritimus*), bearing fruit inside that
closely resembles small garden peas in both appearance and
flavor. After a gourmet luncheon of boiled crab, beach peas, and
raspberry-stuffed rose hips we set off on further explorations.

At high tide we stood on a steep foreshore and cast our fish-
lines into the sea, catching all the foot-long cummer (*Tauto-
golabrus adsperus*) and tautog (*Tautoga onitis*) we could use.
When our easy success made the sport pall, we resumed exploring the vegetation of the island. On a low flat near the sea we

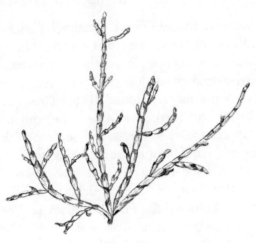

Glasswort.

found orach (*Atriplex*), glasswort (*Salicornia*), and sea blite (*Suaeda*) growing, all relatives of our domestic spinach, and all three good as raw salads or cooked vegetables. Nearby stood a growth of sea rocket (*Cakile*), a plant of the mustard family. Its leaves make a pungent condiment with a horse-radish flavor that is an ideal accompaniment to seafood. Up the hill, among abandoned sea gull nests, we found a luxuriant stand of sheep sorrel (*Rumex acetosella*). Its sour leaves have a lemon-like flavor that makes it, also, a good food to eat with gifts from the sea.

To the little girl who was with us, Gretchen, goes the credit for discovering a small chokecherry tree (*Prunus virginiana*) that was bending to the ground under its weight of ripe fruit. That evening we had a great supper of clam chowder, boiled and buttered orach, and, for dessert, a hot, sweet chokecherry soup, made after the manner of Scandinavian fruit soups, and so delicious that it seemed almost sinful to indulge oneself so. The fish were cleaned and filleted, then put on ice for a fried fish breakfast.

New adventures made each day full and satisfying, and none of us suffered a moment of boredom during the week. I directed the children's attention to the wonders of sea and land, and saw to it that they were brought into a meaningful relationship with the nature all about them. This was accomplished most easily when our discoveries were edible—as they often were.

We turned over rocks at low tide and caught the tiny, slippery, slithery, fluttering eels found there. These were cleaned, dipped in batter and fried, yielding a wonderful fish that was even more appreciated because it had some of the aspects of manna from heaven. The spiny sea urchins were dissected and the orange-colored roe removed. This was cooked in milk, as one makes oyster stew, and was as delicate a dish as we ever tasted. We even gathered the fat periwinkles (*Littorina*) crawling among the seaweed, boiled them in salt water, then lifted the meat from the shells with a toothpick and popped them straight into our mouths, the children's prejudice against eating snail-like creatures completely disappearing in this atmosphere. We gathered Irish moss (*Chondrus crispus*) and boiled it to make a jellied aspic salad filled with wild greens. Quantities of dulse (*Rhodymenia palmata*), another edible seaweed, were dried in the sun and thereafter carried with us for savory snacks while on our explorations.

Our ingestion of nature became our passport into nature study, and one creature or plant led us on to another. Mark and Gretchen learned more botany, zoology, and natural history in that one short week than they would have in a year's classroom work on the same subjects. I was careful to see that each element of nature that came to their attention was brought into a meaningful, pleasurable relationship with them, so the learning went deep. Neither has forgotten a single plant or creature we made use of on our little Robinson Crusoe island.

In contrast to this wonderful experience, another leaps to mind that illustrates why a camper should go slow in buying all that tempting camping equipment. We especially like shadberries for the delicate almond flavor they give to muffins, so when the season for these wild berries arrived, my wife and I put some rudimentary camping gear and preserving equipment in our panel truck and set out in search of shadbushes. We found them in abundance near a public campground, and moved in. We didn't even own a tent, but devised an insect- and weatherproof shelter from a piece of plastic and some mosquito nets saved from Army-surplus jungle hammocks. We could lie in our transparent shelter at night and study the stars.

On the neighboring campsite was one of the most elaborate camps I had ever seen. Its owner told me that he was determined his kids would never suffer the deprivation and discomforts he had known as a boy, and that he wanted to give them the experience of going camping in style. And "style" it was—a three-room, two-toned tent, with a separate screen-house kitchen. The camp beds were softer than those I sleep on at home, the gasoline stove had an oven, and there was a kerosene-powered refrigerator. Even the path to the camp was stylishly marked with poles bearing small red kerosene lanterns that made it gay at night.

That evening I was processing canned shadberries over my campfire when a boy from this fancy camp wandered over. He accepted a handful of sweet shadberries and was thrilled to the core when told that this delicious fruit could be gathered from wild bushes. He carefully looked over our primitive camping arrangements, then sighed, "I wish I could live like this. This is really camping out!"

3. Wild Parties, Boy Scout Style

I RECENTLY returned from Schiff Scout Reservation, located in the beautiful hill country of north central New Jersey. I was helping conduct a seminar on wild foods and survival. It was attended by 150 adult Scout leaders, mostly heads of district councils and Scoutmasters. They ranged in age from early twenties to late fifties, and there were plenty of gray heads, but a group of boys of Scouting age could not have been more enthusiastic.

Friday evening we introduced our subject and showed a film which illustrates a number of ways of having grand fun with wild foods. These include a survival trip, where I took some boys out into the countryside and lived almost solely on wild foods for a week; a semi-survival trip where basic staples are carried along but wild foods must be gathered to make an interesting diet; and then a wild party, or wild banquet, where wild foods are gathered and prepared into gourmet dishes in a kitchen and served at banquet tables.

After whetting the men's appetites with these motion-sound

pictures we showed about a hundred slides of wild foods that could be found right in the area where we were meeting.

Next morning we started actually demonstrating. Frank Jason and Cliff Silva are both dedicated Scout leaders from New Bedford, Massachusetts, and both are real experts at wild food. I am very proud of the fact that it was my book *Stalking the Wild Asparagus* that first interested these two fine men in this subject. Throughout the year they gather and store in their freezers dozens of kinds of wild foods, then pack it in dry ice and bring it to this annual seminar. It was a wild smorgasbord that we served that day. All the food was spread out and explained, cooked, and eaten. Everyone sampled everything—cattail pollen pancakes dipped in cat brier syrup, two dozen different kinds of wild vegetables, and many other delicious morsels that can be had for the taking by anyone armed with a little knowledge and the right spirit.

That morning before breakfast, Frank Jason and I had taken our fishing rods to Lake Therese, the lake on the reservation, and had landed about fifty little panfish, mostly bluegills and perch. I was busy demonstrating the many ways such small fish could be used, from just scaling and beheading and roasting them on a stick over a campfire, to filleting them, dipping the small fillets in Japanese tempura batter, and frying them in deep fat for wild banquets.

We also gathered fresh samples of the dozens of wild foods available in May right on the reservation. These furnished more cooked vegetables and some very good fresh salads.

Between trips to the smorgasbord to fuel the inner man, our guests learned how to cook without utensils and make traps and snares, so in an emergency they could be sure of a wild meat course. They were shown how to make fishing gear that actually will catch fish by improvising a pole out of a tiny sharpened twig and a line from a few threads raveled from an undershirt. They were also taught how to make shelters to protect themselves from rain or cold, with no more tools than a single jackknife.

We explained the clever dovetail notch with which any two pieces of wood can be fastened together to make tools, shelters, camp furniture, and many other conveniences of a survival camp.

All these survival operations, except for the food department, were directed by Kenneth Cole, who is probably the foremost all-round survival expert in the country today. I don't mean that if he were lost in the woods he could eat better than I in the same situation. But I might freeze or die of exposure while he was lying around in comfort in a snug shelter he had improvised. If I ever plan to get lost, I want to get lost with Ken Cole. Then he can furnish housing, traps, tools, furniture, utensils, and other conveniences while I dig up and cook the food. We might just decide to stay lost.

That evening the group seemed most concerned with the safety of wild foods. I explained that no one knows all the poisonous wild plants, not even Dr. John M. Kingsbury, the greatest expert on wild foods in this country, who wrote the best available book on the subject, *Poisonous Plants of the United States and Canada.* You don't have to know any of the poisonous plants in order to pick wild food safely. What you must know is the plant you are picking and eating, and you *must* be able to recognize it unmistakably as an edible plant.

In my mail at home, I often receive what I have come to call "poisonous letters." They go something like this: "I am very much interested in eating weeds and other wild stuff, but how do I tell the poisonous ones from the edible ones?"

I'm sure that these folks have a mental picture of me eating a plateful of some strange wild food, then settling back and waiting to see whether I live or die. Obviously, I don't do it that way, or I would not be here healthily pounding this typewriter. I do not just run through the woods and graze. I never eat a wild plant until I have identified it for certain and know it to be edible. I eat only certain species of wild plants, and I recognize, know, and trust these in the same way that you know and trust the domestic garden vegetables that you eat.

Primitive man long ago learned which wild plants were edible and which were not, I told our guests. Such knowledge, though no longer widely distributed, has not been entirely lost, and I, for one, have dedicated much of my life to collecting and recording as much of it as I can for the use of moderns who would like to get back to a more natural way of living and eating.

Later that evening I was asked whether one can get adequate nutrition from wild plants. In all tests that have been made, wild plants proved much richer in vitamins and minerals than their domestic counterparts. A skillful forager, lost in the woods for a week, will usually have better nutrition than he would at home eating the devitalized and preservative-filled foods that are sold in the average supermarket.

On Sunday morning we had a home-grown church service, which is no great trick in such a gathering. It is amazing how many ministers, deacons, and lay preachers are involved in Scouting. They were sensitive to the situation, and I'm sure God smiled when he saw how much our outdoor worship resembled a pagan, nature-worship ceremony. I approved. I know no way of loving God more than loving His creation.

After worship the remainder of the morning was spent in field trips around the lush, bountiful woods, fields, and streams of Schiff Reservation. My group found about thirty different edible wild plants in one hour. These included burdock, which furnishes three different foods. The long root of first-year plants is an excellent vegetable, beloved by the Japanese. But the Japanese have overlooked two other excellent foods offered by this common dooryard weed. The leaf-stems, in May, will peel, and most of the bitter taste comes off with the shreddy peel. These peeled leaf-stems can be boiled, and taste something like stewed celery. They are even better parboiled and dipped into a fritter batter and fried. This is a hearty dish, and one could easily make a good lunch from it and a salad of wild plants. Best of all is the fat bloom stalk, which appears in June. This must be gathered when it first springs up, before the leaves on the stalk get completely unfolded, and long before the flower buds appear. Even

this early it is sometimes two inches in diameter and two feet
tall. Peel off every bit of the bitter green rind, exposing the white
interior. Slice this crosswise and cook in any way you would
cook potato slices: boil, fry, bake, or put around a roast. It
somewhat resembles potato in flavor, but does not cook apart.
Everyone likes it. The day-lilies growing everywhere contribute
four foods. Any time of the year you can dig beneath the plants
and find a great cluster of little tubers. They are excellent boiled
and buttered. The young stalks, when only a few inches high,
can be cut below the ground, the leaves stripped off and the light
yellow-green heart sliced into a salad or cooked like asparagus.
Cooked, it is one of the sweetest of all vegetables, and I have yet
to meet a person who did not like it. Later, the bloom buds are
very good cooked and served exactly as one would treat green
beans. Finally, the open blossoms can be dipped into a fritter
batter and fried to make a delicate luncheon dish. The buds can
be dried to add to soups, stews, and roasts, making one of the
finest flavoring herbs I have ever tasted. They are mucilaginous
and thicken a stew or soup as okra will. Great for a wild gumbo
if you can find some crayfish and a few sassafras leaves. Add a
bit of wild onion, too. Even the old, dried yesterday's blooms
can be chopped and added to soups and stew with profit. We
found plenty of wild onion, sassafras, and crayfish at Schiff.

We saw wild mustard, good for salad greens, cooked vegetables, or even for seed, to make a hot condiment to accompany
wild game. There were small sprouts of Japanese knotweed that
look like asparagus spears but taste like rhubarb. I've even made
pies of these. Indian cucumber and spring beauty filled the
woods, and both these have highly edible tubers. However, since
using them destroys the plants, I advised that these two beautiful
wild flowers be let strictly alone except for dire emergencies.
There were great patches of wild garlic mustard, whose name
exactly describes its flavor. There simply is no better leaf to add
to a liverwurst sandwich on rye. It is also edible raw or cooked
as an emergency food or at a wild banquet.

Day-lily.

Japanese Knotweed.

May apples were showing off their creamy-white blossoms, but already one could see the tiny fruits in the middle of each bloom which will ripen, in August or September, into one of the finest of wild fruits. Cherries, blackberries, strawberries, raspberries, elderberries, and many other wild fruits were also blossoming, indicating the plenty to come. Everyone was astounded at the abundance of foods to be found all about us. I'm sure the enthusiasm I observed will communicate itself to others, and that the future will see crops of Scouts with an even deeper knowledge of how to live more intimately with nature, and an enriched desire to conserve and beautify our land.

4. Playing Indian

ONE of my most pleasant experiences was a week of semi-survival camping with two boys, both fourteen years old. Mark, whom I have mentioned, had been with me on several trips and was already an expert at foraging wild foods. But Charlie was new at the game. Charlie's mother had grave apprehensions about her boy's subsisting on "weeds" for a week. She warned me that he was a fussy eater. However, he seemed very eager to try the experiment of gathering his living from the wild.

The boys arrived on a Sunday evening in July, and we had a meeting to set up the ground rules. This trip was strictly for fun, so we didn't set quite as rugged restrictions as I have on some past wild-food trips. We agreed to carry biscuit mix, cooking oil, salt, and raw sugar, but these civilized supplies were to be used only in conjunction with wild foods. We would not allow ourselves, for instance, to make pancakes and sugar syrup from the flour and sugar, but we could use the flour as a coating for fish we caught, the oil to fry it in, and the sugar to sweeten a wild-fruit sauce. At the same time I also broke the news that a writer and photographer from one of the big picture magazines would be following us for the first day.

We loaded our gear into the station wagon that evening, tied Mark's little eight-foot boat on top of the car, and left next morning without having breakfast.

In a mile or so, we came on an old field filled with wild black raspberries in the prime of ripeness and halted for breakfast. The boys soon had a bucketful of berries, while I gathered white umbels of elderberry blossoms from a nearby elder bush. We broke out the cooking gear, pumped up the camp stove, and soon had a tasty breakfast ready. Mixing a batter of biscuit mix and water, we dipped in sprigs of elderberry blossoms, then fried them to a golden-brown to make some of the best fritters ever tasted. We boiled a potful of raspberries, strained them through a piece of cheesecloth, then returned the juice to the fire, sweetened to taste, and thickened it slightly with biscuit mix that first had been stirred into cold water to make a paste. When it had cooked long enough to remove the raw, starchy taste of the flour, we had another Scandinavian-style fruit soup that was an ideal accompaniment for the fritters.

Before leaving this old field we came on a great patch of burdock, just putting up its stout bloom stalks. We gathered a supply of these young, tender stalks, peeled away the bitter rind, and put them in a plastic bag for future reference. We also lingered long enough to gather a supply of the black raspberries to take along. Then we drove over a country road until we came to three wild sweet cherry trees with the fruit just right—so another plastic bucket was filled. A patch of orange day-lilies next tempted us, and we stuffed a bag with the green buds, which as I mentioned, taste not only as good as, but better than, green beans. Then we went for poke sprouts. It was really too late for good poke sprouts, but I had a secret; I knew an old brush pile that was surrounded with luxuriant poke. I had gathered the sprouts there in June, cutting the plants back to ground level. This had forced the huge perennial roots to put up new sprouts, and these were now just right. We took all we could use.

It was getting near noon, so we pulled off beside a creek. Mark waded into the shallow stream with a minnow net and began scooping up crayfish, while Charlie and I unlimbered our spinning rods and began fishing a deeper pool. We caught a dozen little spotted rock bass, or calicoes, about seven inches long, and five chain pickerel about ten inches long. There were other treasures. In a little side stream I discovered a nice bed of watercress, and as we were gathering it, Mark spotted a small thicket of wild red currants, not plentiful, but we did manage to find about a cupful.

Our lunch was a thing of beauty. I lined up our plates on a fallen log and on each I put a helping of peeled and boiled poke sprouts, looking a bit like asparagus but tasting better; some thin-sliced boiled burdock flower stalks, a little like potatoes but far more tasty; and a hot browned pickerel, garnished with watercress. To make an aromatic tea, we poured boiling water over a handful of spicebush twigs.

After lunch we began gathering the ingredients for a wild salad we would enjoy that evening. We returned to the watercress bed and restocked, then gathered cattail hearts along the stream. This means pulling young cattail plants from the mother-rhizome, cutting off the bottom four inches of each stalk, then peeling this base down to a white heart that can easily be pinched in two with the thumbnail. These make a good vegetable either raw or cooked, but in a salad they furnish a snow-white crispness that has the flavor of cucumber. We also found a patch of sheep sorrel with its tender leaves that taste like lemon. Near a seepy spring we found an abundance of wild mint. Some patches have a weedy flavor, but this had a clear and pure spearmint taste. The salad was growing. Our camp icebox was getting stuffed with bags of wild plants.

We carried everything to a pure mountain spring to wash it all, then the boys cut and mixed the salad. It needed no vinegar, thanks to the sheep sorrel, so they concocted a good dressing of oil, salt, and a hint of wild garlic. It tasted just as good as it

Sheep Sorrel.

looked, glowing with nature's goodness in a huge wooden bowl.

That night, I poached some finely diced fillets of rock bass, mixed them with a generous portion of the celebrated salad, and cooked some pitted cherries with sugar and little crescent-shaped dumplings. By the time we had finished this excellent dinner darkness had fallen. We were tired, but happy and well filled, so the sleeping bags felt good.

Next morning, while the boys slept, I went fishing in the pond. On a long cast I caught a tiny bluegill, and as I was winding him in a big bass took him. I opened the bail and let the bass run. When it stopped, I waited until I was sure the bluegill was swallowed, then struck, and had about three pounds of dynamite on the line. Mark soon joined me, and we developed a technique. We would bait with a worm, drop it right against the bank where the tiny bluegills congregated, and would soon have a two- or three-inch bluegill on the hook. This was then cast out to deep water, and as soon as a bass saw the bluegill, obviously in trouble, he would take him. Then by the waiting process we would soon have the bass firmly on the hook. In about an hour we both had our limit, eight apiece, of nice fifteen-inch large-mouth bass.

With such a wealth of fish there was no need to be economical, so we reduced them to boneless fillets, browning some for breakfast and eating huge bowls of fresh black raspberries. Charlie showed no signs of being a fussy eater. His only food peculiarity seemed to be a desire for the good things we were eating in very large helpings. Gathering one's own food from the wild seems to be a sure and instant cure for feeding problems. I have often observed that not only will a child eat food he has helped to gather from the wild and prepare from scratch, but everyone else around must eat it also if they want to keep his friendship.

After breakfast we gathered cattail hearts, sprouts, and rhizomes for future supplies. We also collected a bag of milkweed buds, which can be cooked like broccoli, and protected by a pair of plastic gloves, I peeled a number of thistle bloom stalks which when young and tender are delicious boiled. With our camp icebox nearly bursting, there was little need to forage for more food, and the boys asked me if we could retreat farther into the wilderness. They had been studying a map of the huge forested mountain area to the north and west of us, and wanted to get into wilder country. I agreed, so we struck camp and packed up, then headed for the hills. It was decided to park the car in an area none of us had ever explored, lock up all food supplies, take only our cooking gear—and then see if we could scrape together a decent lunch from nature alone.

We followed a narrow dirt road, shown on none of our maps, until we came to its end, with a shallow creek on one side and a rocky hill on the other. Charlie put some plastic bags in his pocket and started climbing the hill, while Mark and I waded into the stream. In the clear water crayfish scuttled around the rocks in reverse gear. We soon found that they could be captured by swift and fearless grabs. It's true that some of them managed to nip our fingers, and we both made tiny blood donations, but this small risk turned a task into sport. We also discovered numerous freshwater clams half buried in the creek bottoms. Mark was so fascinated by this underwater life that I couldn't get him to stop collecting them even when I judged we had all the crayfish and clams that we could eat.

I crossed the creek and began searching the woods and banks. At a wet, springy place I found some bulbous spring cress (*Cardamine bulbosa*). It was already covered with white blossoms, and the leaves were far too bitter to eat this late in the season. But I pulled up a dozen of them where they were growing too thickly for their own good, to get the tender, bulbous roots about an inch in diameter. These have a mild horseradish flavor that would be delicious with crayfish.

Nearby, I found a great patch of Indian cucumber (*Medeola virginiana*). This is a little plant not more than a foot high with a slender, single stem and two whorls of leaves, like a small umbrella over a larger one, with a spidery yellow flower atop the upper whorl. These were also growing too thickly, so I liberated a few dozen of the snow-white roots the size and shape of my little finger, crisp and tender, with a pronounced garden cucumber flavor.

I almost had to drag Mark out of the stream to help me build a fire, wash our tubers, steam the clams, and boil the crayfish. By the time we had things well started, Charlie came back, all excited. He had found low bushes bearing large Juneberries, or shadberries (*Amelanchier canadensis*), on top of the ridge. He had gathered about a quart of these oversized berries and had also filled another plastic bag with sour grass (*Oxalis acetosella*), which has clover-shaped leaves with a lemon-like flavor.

We had an excellent lunch. The boiled crayfish, shelled and

Sour Grass.

deveined, were far more delicious than the finest shrimp, and when eaten with the slightly pungent cress bulbs and the acid oxalis leaves, they were delightful. The clams—well, they were edible, if one wants to stretch the word. A really hungry man would probably appreciate them, and I think they would make a pretty good chowder if one added enough bacon, onions, and potatoes. But just steamed they were far from being one of the best things I ever tasted. Maybe it was just in contrast to those luxurious crayfish that they tasted so plebeian. We searched all the shells, unsuccessfully, for pearls, for these freshwater clams, or mussels as they are sometimes called, do occasionally produce some valuable stones, but it wasn't our day. We left the clam meat near the stream where the raccoons, whose tracks covered the muddy banks with hieroglyphics, could find it.

The possession of so much food gave us a new freedom, so we went for a drive in the mountains, strictly for sightseeing. Following a dim dirt road, we came on an old abandoned sawmill. Growing around it were great patches of pennyroyal, a fragrant, minty plant that makes a fine tea. At the edges of the sawdust piles sassafras sprouts were thick and easily pulled from the loose soil. In the cutover land around the old sawmill, already becoming jungly with second growth, we found wintergreen plants by the ton, some of them still bearing last year's berries. While gathering these beverage materials, we came upon a great abundance of low early blueberries in the prime of ripeness. This was a discovery indeed, and we gathered as many as we'd be able to eat in a week, besides making a second lunch of this sweet, juicy fruit. We decided to camp at a nearby mountain spring to revel in all this goodness.

After pitching camp we had an early dinner of bass baked with wild herbs in aluminum foil, boiled burdock stems that remotely resembled potatoes, and the salad—enhanced now with Indian cucumbers and cress bulbs. I was tired and sought my sleeping bag early, but awakened later to find the two boys eating crayfish by the light of the campfire. The savory odor inspired enough hunger to drive away my sleepiness, so I joined them and we shelled crayfish until the last one had disappeared, then ate large bowls of fresh blueberries.

We spent what remained of the week very pleasantly, fishing, swimming, and boating on the pond, swapping lies with other fishermen who came to wet a line there, gathering wild foods, wading the creek after crayfish, cooking up strange and delicious concoctions, and just plain loafing. Our days were full, and so were we. I can't remember having enjoyed a camping trip more, and it would be very hard to devise a more economical vacation.

I had expected the boys to be hungry for civilized fare by the end of the week, but they were perfectly ready to go on for another week, if I had had the time. Shortly after returning home, Charlie's mother called to tell me that this formerly fussy eater had actually gained about four pounds!

5. Outward Bound

I AM writing this on a small island in an isolated lake located in one of God's show places, Superior National Forest, in northern Minnesota. At the international boundary, this wonderful area of north woods joins up with Quetiquo Provincial Park in Ontario, and together the two parks make up one of the largest roadless, lake-studded wilderness areas left in North America.

Float planes are not allowed to land on these lakes, so the only way to get here is by canoe. No noise and no smell of gasoline disturb the solitude. The only sounds are the natural ones—the northern sparrow singing, the wind in the pine trees, the laughing loon in the distance. Such sounds do not disturb the silence.

This is the kind of camping I preach about. We are a lake, a few short rivers, and five portages from the nearest road. The water is perfectly clear and so pure that if I feel thirsty I merely walk to the lake edge and dip up a drink without the least fear of contamination. Our camping outfit is a light forester's tent, sleeping bags, some simple cooking utensils, food, and a change of clothes. It all fits into one pack—light enough to be carried

across the portages by one man. We travel in pairs, one man
carrying the canoe while the other carries the pack. We have no
camp stove or lantern, but instead use open fires of birch wood or
pine knots to cook and see by. And more than half our food is
grown by nature herself.

Last night a great northern pike took a lure and was landed
right in the frying pan. Wild strawberries picked from an open
shore furnished a breakfast fruit with which no domestic berry
can compare. Fishing this morning yielded only one small walleye, but we made it into a delicious stew, adding cattail hearts,
rock lichens, wild onions, arrowhead tubers, and a great cluster
of oyster mushrooms found growing on a dying birch tree by the
lake's edge. My companion likes oyster mushrooms so well that
he insisted we have them again at dinner, this time rolled in corn
meal and French-fried to a golden crispness.

On the island where we are camped, serviceberries or Juneberries are showing signs of ripening, while blueberries by the
ton are swelling on the plants. Last evening we lay awhile on a
thick carpet of pine needles watching a magnificent display of
the Northern Lights, and felt no need of television, transistor
radios, or other accouterments of civilization.

It is hard to believe that I am here to work, actually being
paid to savor the wilderness in this wonderful way. On the
southern edge of all this wilderness is the Minnesota Outward
Bound School, a unit of one of the most inspired educational
institutions I have ever encountered.

Here young men and women are separately given a very fun-
damental sort of training through a creative encounter with the
wilderness. At the camp headquarters they take intensive
courses in canoeing, drown-proofing, physical conditioning,
ropes, map-reading and use of compass, first aid, rock climbing,
ecology, and wilderness survival.

The canoe has been basic transportation in this watery wilderness since prehistoric times, so the students are trained to be
perfectly at home with this light and beautiful boat. They learn

not only all the possible canoe strokes, but also how to handle the canoe under all conditions of weather and water—portaging, shooting rapids, recovering from a swamping, and traveling through wind and waves. In this training-by-doing they quickly come to appreciate the difference between sensible courage and foolhardiness, for the school will not tolerate violations of good safety practices by the more reckless students.

Drown-proofing is a method of teaching water safety designed to make the students secure in the water under any condition, even fatigue, cramps, or panic. Physical conditioning is done through calisthenics, and all the training they receive here contributes to making the students' bodies strong, supple, and agile, so they can be as much at home in the wilderness as the deer or any wild creature. In a ropes course they learn enough balance, timing, agility, and aerial judgment to enable any one of them to understudy Tarzan.

The use of maps and compass is learned on treks and shake-down expeditions. On treks students are taken out, shown where they are on a detailed map, then told to make their way back to camp through trackless wilderness. Shakedown expeditions consist of overnight canoe cruises to nearby lakes by routes which involve rivers, streams, lakes, rapids, and portages, going in one way and coming out another.

In ecology students learn the geographical and biological history of the area, and the relationship between the living things that inhabit it, and even how they themselves can fit into the picture in a non-destructive way. This is the best conservation and anti-littering training that I know. In rock climbing they learn the lines, knots, techniques, and nomenclature used by experienced mountain climbers and experience the thrill of getting up otherwise unclimbable rock faces and rappelling over sheer cliffs. Here they learn a healthy respect for the hazards nature offers and come to appreciate that their safety depends on perfect cooperation with fellow students.

I'm here to teach the wilderness survival course. Just now,

between courses, I am making a survey of the wild food possibilities near some of the lakes over which our students travel. If I had tried to design an ideal vacation, I could not possibly have chosen one more enjoyable. It seems my destiny to be paid for doing the things I most enjoy.

I endeavor to train the students in the recognition and use of the wild foods that nature so generously offers in this section. It's not done in a classroom, but right on the lakes and streams and in the forest. They learn by actually gathering, preparing, cooking, and eating these delicacies.

Despite all these outdoor activities and the fact that the program runs only during the summer months, this is not just another summer camp. It is a school, but like none other ever seen. This vast canoe wilderness furnishes the challenge, the teaching materials, and the examination papers.

The big test comes with a long expedition of two weeks or more. By canoe on streams, rivers, and lakes, and over portages, the students travel in brigades of twelve, far up into the Canadian wilderness, camping on lake shores and islands. These trips feature night canoeing exercises, running rapids and doing other white-water work, forced paddles over long distances, and the training that comes from having to live in intimacy with eleven other students and two instructors, from many different backgrounds.

The climax of these expeditions comes with the solo survival test, when each student is marooned—all alone—on some lake or promontory, with a minimum of equipment and no food whatever, and has to live three days and nights on the bounty that nature can provide for those who approach her with knowing eyes and a humble spirit. Many of the students are genuinely surprised to discover that their training has transformed a menacing enemy into a friendly and hospitable mother.

Providing for merely physical needs is comparatively easy in the wilderness if one has received the proper training, so the big challenge comes from coping with loneliness and one's own lack of inner resources. Some students suffer on solo, some do very well, and some have a ball—but all agree that these three days of solitude furnish a soul-shaking and intensely meaningful experience.

In all this learning-by-doing the students acquire new knowledge at amazing speed. The one short month this course takes has an impact on lives that is out of all proportion to the time it takes. Not only do the students learn new skills, but learn to live in greater harmony with nature, with their fellow men, and—most important of all—with themselves.

6. Outward Bound Again

AFTER the publication of my first article on the Outward Bound School of Minnesota, I received a flood of inquiries about the school. Actually twenty-four such schools are scattered throughout the world, five of them in the United States. (If you would like more complete information on any or all, write to Outward Bound, Inc., Andover, Mass. 01810, and mention this book.)

My first contact with Outward Bound came in the spring of 1965, in a letter from the director of Hurricane Island Outward Bound School located in Penobscot Bay, Maine, which was just getting started at that time. Where the Minnesota School uses the forest to furnish the needed challenge, teaching materials, and examination papers, the Hurricane Island School uses the ocean. My love of the wilderness is exceeded only by my love of the sea, so of course I was interested. The director there had read my books *Stalking the Wild Asparagus* and *Stalking the Blue-Eyed Scallop*, and hoped I could help the school in the solo-survival program. He proposed to put a yacht and crew at my disposal and have me cruise among the small uninhabited islands off that part of coastal Maine, fishing, digging clams, and exploring wild foods available. What a job!

Needless to say, I jumped at this opportunity, and I had a glorious time. I not only wrote a little textbook for the school's use in its training, but became so interested that I decided to neglect my writing for the summer and stay as a teacher.

The first lot of students, ninety-six young men, sixteen to twenty years old, soon arrived and plunged into the grueling, demanding course. My classroom was the beaches, forests, and clearings of Hurricane Island, and the boys learned by actually gathering, preparing, and eating wild foods during the class sessions. Hurricane proved to be an ideal island for this activity, having on it nearly all the wild foods that could be found anywhere in the area. By extremely careful conservation, we managed to keep it continuously productive, and it is as lush today as it was when we started, although by now over a thousand students have gathered, cooked, and sampled its wild delicacies.

A few days after the first month-long course started, I overheard a very apt description of myself. I was walking on one of the woodland trails and overtook two students walking on the same trail. I was wearing sneakers, and as I moved noiselessly up behind them I heard my name mentioned. I cocked an ear —with a little dread, for an eavesdropper never hears any good about himself. The one who had not mentioned my name hadn't yet sorted out the faculty, and he asked, "Just which one is Euell Gibbons?" The other answered, "Oh you know. He's the prehistoric cat who thinks all this crazy wild stuff is the main scene."

It wasn't long until the students were thinking that the crazy wild stuff *was* the main scene, for solo time comes after only two weeks' training. We took them out in boats and marooned them, each one entirely alone on his private, uninhabited island. We gave them a little get-by equipment—a hunting knife as their only weapon and tool, and a No. 10 can to serve as combination cooking pot and serving dish.

They had two choices—either eat that crazy wild stuff or go hungry. They ate, some of them very well indeed and some not so well. Some loved the solo and some hated it, but all agreed that spending those three days alone on an island had been one of the most important episodes in their lives. One had only to go with the pick-up boat that brought them back to the school and observe the enthusiasm and newly found self-reliance of these boys to be convinced of the importance of this kind of training. Some had appeared pretty small, timid, and forlorn as we dropped them off in the beginning, but three days later, when they were coming off those Robinson Crusoe islands, they were as tall as the spruce trees that grew there. The wonder of it all still glowed in their eyes and vibrated in their voices. They weren't about to listen to what any teacher or anyone else had to say at this time. They wanted to tell anyone who would listen about the soul-shaking experiences they had had in solitude.

We had three groups of students that summer, and I experienced the joy and grief, the many triumphs and the few disappointments, that are the lot of all teachers. It was the August group that really challenged me. After returning from their solos, they consulted together and then sent a delegation to talk to me. Their first question was, "Mr. Gibbons, did you ever go on a solo?" I glibly explained that I had been on several survival trips in this same area and had lived as long as one week on nothing but wild food. They then wanted to know if I had done this all alone, and how much equipment I had taken along. I had to admit that I had always had companions and had never deliberately tried to limit myself on equipment.

It was their unanimous opinion that I had never been on a survival trip that could fairly be compared to their solo experiences, and furthermore, they believed I should go on such a solo immediately.

I don't think there was any malice in their insistence. It wasn't a case of "you go out and suffer as we did." They felt that something of tremendous importance had happened to them on these solitary exiles, and they wanted me to share it so we could better communicate. They were convinced that I had missed the very heart-meat of the experience by never doing it alone. They knew that in those three days they had changed their attitudes toward nature, and their role in nature, they had seen themselves with new eyes, and had also altered opinions of their fellow students, their teachers, and sometimes their parents and many others, and they wanted to see how this conversion-experience would affect me. I think they also wanted to see how a professional would handle the problems that plagued them. They wanted to see the prehistoric cat strut his stuff.

It was easily arranged since, with their return, my teaching job was finished until the next batch of students arrived. I consented to have them select the island on which I was to be exiled, inspect my gear to see that I carried no contraband (as I had done with them), decide at what time I was to be dropped off, then pick me up at the end of three days and debrief me as I had debriefed them to decide how well I had done.

They chose a hunk of granite called Bald Island, waited until the lunch bell rang, then rushed me into the boat without lunch. On the way to the island they went over my gear, removing a ball of twine with which I had intended to make a crab net and a paper packet of sugar that just happened to be in my shirt pocket. A few minutes later I had stepped from the boat to a flat rock, was waving goodbye to them and, unexpectedly, I was feeling a sort of mild panic at the thought of being absolutely alone the next three days.

The weather was fine, so I decided I would explore my little paradise before selecting a campsite and rigging some sort of shelter. The island covered seven or eight acres and was almost two islands, being shaped like an hourglass. One end had been quarried for granite to build grimy cities during the last century, and contained a sizable marsh where the quarry had been. I was delighted to see that this marsh was grown up in cattails, and even more elated when I found near one edge of the marsh a tiny spring of clear, cold water. It was sure to be pure on this uninhabited island, for it is man who pollutes water and makes it unusable by man.

Near the shore were several large patches of wild roses which grow wild, like a weed, on these Maine islands, and these were bearing plum-sized rose hips that taste like a rather poor grade of mealy apple. Nearby were some scattered canes of wild red raspberries, not in any great abundance but I could tell they would ripen about as many berries as I could use each day. I started my lunch at the wrong end by having dessert first, eating all the rose hips and raspberries I wanted. Next I found, just above high-tide level, several green patches of orach, the seaside relative of the spinach and Swiss chard we raise in our gardens, and a better plant than either of them. The leaves are fleshy, tender, and tasty, and also mildly salted. In the same area I found two related plants, sea blite and glasswort, both salty, tender vegetables that can be eaten raw or cooked. Then I spied rocket, a member of the mustard family with a pungent horse-radish flavor that hardly needs a salad dressing. I laid all four kinds in layers in my hand, like a club sandwich, and nibbled this instant salad as I continued my explorations.

No birch trees grew on my island, but among the debris thrown up by past storms was some birch driftwood, from which I peeled some dry birch bark to use as kindling in starting my campfires, for I had but eight matches for the three days. Also among this flotsam grew beach peas with clusters of peas sticking up as if asking someone to pick them. I obliged, filling my pockets for a shelling bee when I decided to rest. These are almost as good as garden peas.

On top of the bald hill that gave the island its name, I found sour sorrel, which would be a good relish with the seafood I expected to get as soon as the tide went out. Here I also found a pretty good patch of skunk currants with dead-ripe fruit. Despite that name, which puts most people off, these currants are fairly palatable when eaten by the handful, and one doesn't notice the skunky odor after the first bite.

Satisfied that the island would support me, I returned to the isthmus that separated the two ends of the island to pitch my camp. I gathered dead grass by the armload, made a deep bed of it, pitched a 7-by-10-foot piece of plastic over it as a tent, and was snug as an eider duck in its down nest.

The tremendous tide of Maine had been flowing out ever since I landed, and the seaweed-covered granite that formed the island's skirts now stood bare. It was time to raid Neptune's larder. There were acres of blue mussels, an excellent shellfish, but one that should not be eaten too often or too greedily, for it soons palls if eaten in any great quantity. Manna from heaven should come in fifty-seven varieties, and usually does if one has the knowledge to recognize them. Huge periwinkles snailed about the seaweed-covered rocks at low-tide level. These are considered very good eating in many parts of the world, although few Americans seem to know that they are edible. I have a passion for their delicious seafood flavor. There were literally thousands of sea urchins (*Strongylocentrotus drobachiensis*) crowding the rocks just under the low water, within reachable distance. When broken open each three-inch-round green urchin yields about half an ounce of orange-colored, five-parted roe with a flavor that is more delicate and delicious than that of caviar.

I disliked the idea of having to wait until low tide to gather such goodies, so I decided to domesticate several kinds of creatures. I found a crate among the driftwood piles, filled it with mussels, periwinkles, and sea urchins, then moved them to a higher tide pool where they would be available whenever I was hungry. As I was carrying the crate up the shore I stepped on a little patch of gravel and saw a squirt. I immediately set the crate down and started scratching gravel. It was a virgin clam bed, never robbed before, and the steamer clams were packed against one another. I removed three dozen from a hole containing less than one cubic foot of gravel, using nothing but my hands to dig.

That evening I dined on steamed clams, boiled beach peas, and a mixed vegetable salad; then I strolled through the roses, raspberries, and currants for dessert. Later I rigged a handline, and when the tide had rolled back in I stood by a steep shore and caught four harbor pollack, not the best fish in the world, but perfectly edible. A cold fog had swept in by this time, so I cleaned the pollack and laid them on a cold rock to eat for breakfast. I had my little plastic tent tightly closed, but two mosquitoes got in as I did. Did you ever notice that not all mosquitoes hum in the same key? One was a high tenor, while the other one harmonized perfectly with the deep bass foghorn I could hear in the distance. I couldn't seem to hit them in the dark, so I finally just bared an arm and let them fill up, hoping they would go to sleep and let me do the same.

I awoke shortly after daybreak and the first thing I saw was the mosquitoes, swelled with my blood, hanging upside down on my low ceiling. I got revenge and left two bloody splotches on the plastic. Then I became aware that some sea gulls were making an awful racket nearby. My fish! I leaped from bed and ran out just in time to see a gull swallow the last of the cleaned fish and fly off giving his jackass cry. I shouted curses into the air after the thief, then breakfasted very well on steamed sea urchin roe, which tastes a bit like scrambled eggs with muskmelon, flavors that blend surprisingly well together.

That day I never knew when breakfast ended and lunch started, nor when lunch was finished and dinner begun; I just kept cooking and eating all day. This heroic eating wasn't dictated by hunger, for I never became the least bit hungry during my three days on the island. However, I was already envisioning the debriefing the students would give me when I returned. They would expect me to make maximum use of all the resources the island provided, so I determined I would eat everything edible that could be found. It became a drag. I was eating far more than I wanted. Altogether I ate over twenty-five kinds of wild food in those three days, and I gained three pounds.

When I went up the hill to eat some more skunk currants, I found a large expanse of rock covered with clam shells, mussel shells, crab shells, lobster shells, and sea urchin tests. I immediately recognized it as a sea gull drop, where the gulls drop their loot onto the rocks to break open the shells so they can get at the meat. While there I saw a sea gull coming with a large crab. I quickly hid behind a bayberry bush, and when the gull let go of the crab I broke cover, screaming at the top of my voice and waving my arms like a madman. Such antics scared the gull off and I got the big crab, then hid again. Soon another gull appeared with another crab, and the whole performance was repeated. By the time the screaming had made me hoarse I had four big crabs. I carried them home, blushing to remember how I had cursed the sea gulls as thieves that very morning.

I still had all the clams, mussels, sea urchins, and periwinkles I could use, but I couldn't stay off the shore at low tide, so I went down to see what lived under the rocks at low-water level. Nearly every rock I turned over had one to six tiny eels under it, from three to six inches long. These are the slipperiest and wigglingest creatures alive, but I did get a few dozen of them into my cooking can. I noticed some small green crabs under the rocks, too, and when I touched one, I found that he was a recently molted soft-shell. These little greenies are perfectly good to eat, but so small that it hardly pays to pick the scant meat from hard-shelled ones. However, these soft-shelled crabs were something else. One could merely pull back the soft upper shell, remove the gills, or devil's-fingers, and all the rest of the crab could be cooked and eaten. I gathered a few dozen of them. Using one for bait that night I caught a four-pound cod. Things were going from good to better.

The next day I used clams, mussels, crabs, my fish, sea urchin roe, and all the vegetable foods I could find to make a sort of survivor's bouillabaisse. It could have stood some white wine and French bread, but even without these it was a pretty good stew. I gathered seaweeds and dried them, and when I went to sleep I was still chewing on a cud of dried dulse.

On the last day I decided that I would gather some food to take back to the poor people stranded at the school, who didn't have all these goodies. I gathered rose hips, raspberries, clams, sea urchins and mussels, and when the boat came to pick me up I felt as if I was going on a relief mission to the starving Biafrans.

On my return the boys all gathered in the assembly room to debrief me. After they got my story they went into a huddle and decided that I should receive a barely passing grade. They would have agreed to a higher grade except for one thing: I had been telling them that solo should be a time of serious meditation, deep contemplation, and integrating spiritual experiences, and quite obviously I had thought of very little besides food.

7. An Autobiographical Note

IT seems strange how a completely random correspondence, from widely separated people who have never heard of one another, seems to fall into patterns of similarity. Recently, for instance, I received a number of letters all asking for the same very personal information: "How did you get this way? How did this passion for wild foods originate?"

Another group of letters all come from widely separated points in the Southwest, mainly from Texas, New Mexico, and Arizona. These people want to know what relevance my wild-food articles can have to their semi-arid region. Letters like these always make me smile, for it was in that very section of the country that my wild-food interests originated and developed. I was never out of the Southwest until I reached manhood, and I probably know the native foods of that area better than any other. I decided that both these sets of letters could probably be answered by giving a bit of my background.

Actually, I don't know how I acquired this interest. It has been there from as early as I can remember. The fact that my mother and my maternal grandmother were both excellent, self-trained naturalists, with wide knowledge of the wild foods in the area where they lived, probably helped me to develop this passion—but it didn't make it inevitable. None of my brothers and sisters, who shared this same parent and grandparent, became naturalists. Maybe it was an innate streak of laziness that made the idea of living in harmony with nature—taking the free gifts she had to offer, reaping where I did not sow, eating food that was produced by the sweat of no man's brow—so utterly fascinating.

When people told me that the Indians used to live on wild plants, fruits, berries, nuts, and roots, they never satisfied me. I wanted to know which plants, roots, fruits, and nuts. Did they still grow, and could I find them? If I ate them, would I like them? I found there were very few answers to these questions, so I started a lifelong quest for knowledge about wild foods. I invented my first wild-food recipe when I was five years old by pounding together shelled hickory nuts and sweet hackberries to make a wild candy bar. From the first taste I was hooked.

My early childhood was spent in East Texas, which is not at all like the popular picture that the word "Texas" invokes. It is a country of usually ample rainfall, small farms, sandy land, piny woods, and low hills alternating with hardwood-forested river bottoms. I roamed the woods, fields, and waste places seeking what I might devour. I learned to appreciate wild blackberries and dewberries, wild strawberries, mulberries, mustang grapes, muscadines, wild sandhill plums, black haws, persimmons, pawpaws, a kind of wild passion fruit we called maypops, wild cherries, and many lesser wild nibbles. With my mother or grandmother I gathered a vast array of potherbs for the table, including dandelions, poke greens, lamb's quarters, wild mustard, and peppergrass. In the fall we collected wild pecans and wild black walnuts, hickory nuts, and water chinquapins, as well as digging Jerusalem artichokes, grassnuts, and chufas.

When I was eleven, my parents moved to New Mexico, where

Maypops.

Muscadine.

Russian Thistle.

Prickly Pear.

I devoted myself to studying the wild food of that semi-arid region. That is why I can assure these Southwesterners that their land is not destitute of wild foods. I found several familiar greens there, such as lamb's quarters and peppergrass, and I quickly discovered that the most common weed of that area, the Russian thistle—one of the several plants called the "tumbleweed"—makes an excellent cooked green when gathered young and tender. Among fencerows and field edges it comes up thick as the hair on a dog's back and is best gathered in quantity with a pair of kitchen shears. Cooked only a few minutes in salted water, and heavily buttered, it is better than spinach.

After each rain in the summer, purslane (*Portulaca oleracea*) springs up everywhere. You could gather it by the ton if you had use for so much. This is a triple-threat food plant, the leaves being served raw in salads or cooked like spinach, while the succulent stems make a fine dill pickle. If one throws a large number of plants on a tarpaulin, they quickly seed before dying and supply quite a quantity of black round little seeds. When ground and make into pancakes, these could chase buckwheat cakes right off the table!

Huge areas in the Southwest are covered with prickly pear cactus. I am grateful for this plant, for I believe it was partly responsible for my becoming a good rider. Many's the time I have managed to stay on the back of a bucking mustang simply because there was no place to fall except among those vicious spines.

But this plant has other uses besides encouraging good horsemanship. Although the pear-shaped fruits are covered with clusters of bristle-like stickers, these are easily brushed off by using a bunch of grass or weeds as a whisk broom—and then the fruit is edible. It varies in quality among a number of species, but only through good, better, and superb. In northwestern New Mexico I remember a low species that bore bright-yellow fruit as sweet as sugar. The fruits of most species are red or purple, but whatever the color, this is a fine fruit if properly handled.

The flattened stem sections of the prickly pear, usually called "leaves," make an outstanding vegetable dish. Use a pair of kitchen tongs and a sharp knife to gather them. Take only the recently grown tender "leaves" and cut off all the clusters of stickers. The fleshy "leaf" can then be sliced into tender strips, cooked, seasoned, and served like green beans.

Other cacti are useful. The strawberry cactus, resembling a tiny skinny-barrel cactus, bears delicious fruit that must be treated exactly the same as the prickly pear. Several of the barrel cacti also produce edible fruit. I am especially fond of the purple fruit borne by one small species; it tastes like a juicy fig. The inner pulp of the barrel cactus contains a great deal of water, and has saved the life of more than one desert traveler. This pulp can be cut into cubes, soaked in lime water for twenty-four hours, and then boiled in heavy syrup to make cactus candy, a desert confection. The huge *saguaro* cactus bears an excellent purple fruit, as does the organ-pipe cactus.

There are other fruits in this fascinating land. Along the bottoms of well-watered canyons grow great groves of Western chokecherries (*Prunus Virginiana var. Melanocarpa*), larger, blacker, and less astringent than Eastern chokecherries. I have eaten many pounds of these cherries just as I picked them from the tree. The juice, extracted by simmering the cherries until tender, then straining, makes a dark, rich jelly, with commercial pectin. It's even better when made with half apple juice. We quit using it for jelly, however, when we found that these chokecherries made the finest Scandinavian fruit soup ever tasted. We simply extracted the juice, then canned it, pouring it boiling hot into sterilized jars and sealing with sterilized lids. When we wanted a special treat, we opened a jar, added to the juice one jar of water, the rind of one lemon, and one stick of cinnamon. After twenty minutes of boiling, we strained out the rind and cinnamon, then sweetened it to taste, thickened it slightly with cornstarch, boiled it again until it looked clear, then served it, either hot or cold, as a soup course or as a dessert.

Look in those same canyons for the canyon grape (*Vitis*

arizonica), which makes good grape juice and very fine grape jelly. The very finest jelly timber of the Southwest is furnished by the red-fruited barberry (*Berberis haematocarpa*), locally known by its Spanish name of *algerita*. These are shrubs only a few feet high with prickly, holly-like leaves and blood-red berries in the fall. While very acid, these berries make a jelly that ruins your taste for cranberry sauce. The Oregon grape, another member of the barberry family, has purple berries which make a fair jelly, but it can't be compared to the *algerita*.

The yuccas are often confused with cactus in the popular mind, but they are really members of the lily family. The best of these is the Spanish dagger (*Yucca baccata*) with stiff, fleshy leaves up to four feet long, terminating in fierce spikes. They don't bloom every year, but when they do they furnish several good foods. The bloom stalk, when very young and less than a foot high, can be sliced and cooked through two waters to make a palatable and nourishing vegetable. The fleshy, cream-colored blossoms are good chopped into a tossed salad. The fruits, shaped like a stubby banana, are good roasted while slightly green. Peeled after roasting, they taste a bit like sweet potato. When the fruit is ripe, it is sweet, almost gummy, and very nourishing. Even the thin-leaved bear grass (*Yucca glauca*) furnishes edible flower stalks and flowers, but the fruit is dry and, to my taste, inedible. The root of this plant lathers in water, making a good shampoo. It is often called "soapweed."

There is a wild potato that grows in the hills of New Mexico and Arizona. I don't mean a tame potato gone wild, but a real wild plant, resembling a small potato plant and producing sweet little tubers about the size of grapes. I have often enjoyed these fried, boiled, or roasted. Nodding wild onions make a strong condiment, or, if boiled in several waters, a palatable vegetable. The sego lily is too beautiful a flower to be destroyed for the little food furnished, but it's good to know that, should a dire emergency arise, the starchy bulb of this plant, about the size of a walnut, makes a very palatable dish boiled or roasted.

In the fall after late summer rains, giant puffballs often ap-

Oregon Grape.   Wild Potato.

pear overnight around the juniper trees. These edible fungi are excellent if gathered early, while the flesh is still snow-white, then sliced and fried in butter, diced raw into tossed salads, or dipped into a highly flavored fritter batter and fried in deep fat.

Around sagebrush, look for naked broomrape (that lovely name!) that is parasitic on sagebrush roots. Only the flower stalk, bearing tiny purple tubular flowers, appears above ground, but the underground stem is white and tender, good raw or cooked.

As for nuts, the Southwesterners have the finest and sweetest nut that grows wild in this country—the piñon nut produced by the nut pine (*Pinus edulis*), a low conifer with spreading branches, short needles, and a delightful fragrance. In good piñon years, these nuts can be swept up under the trees with a branch of sagebrush and collected in piles. During poorer years the easiest way to get them is to rob those great pack-rat nests built of sticks, bark, cactus, and junk. I have torn these nests apart and found as many as three quarts of cleaned nuts inside. Slightly roasted, shelled and eaten, they are delightful to the taste and very nourishing. A cupful of shelled nuts, one egg, ½ cup milk, and a little salt blended in an electric blender to a smooth batter makes a very tasty pancake that is so rich it never needs buttering.

Don't cry about your barren land, you Southwesterners—it is more fruitful than you think. I honestly believe that if I picked my route and time of the year, I could walk from the Gulf Coast of Texas, across New Mexico, Arizona, and California, to the Pacific Coast, living entirely on the wild food, and never go hungry!

8. Nibbling at the Edge of a Daring Adventure

ONE December when I took a combination business and pleasure trip to New Mexico and West Texas, that boast about walking the Southwest came to mind, and frankly I wondered if I actually could make it good. I wanted to explore the territory, its wild food, and the possible routes and seasons for such a trek. So I flew to Albuquerque, where my brother and I had some writing tasks to complete. Then we started south in his car. For many hours we drove down the Rio Grande Valley and found that along the river survival would present no difficulties —there are vast fields of cattails, tules, and reeds.

The cattails (*Typha latifolia*) can furnish survival food any time of the year in this section where the ground seldom freezes. In December the stout ropelike rhizomes that underlie such beds of cattails were filled with good eating. Roasted in front of a campfire, the rhizomes taste like a fibrous sweet potato and are a great energy food. The raw rhizomes, peeled and dried, can

Cattail.

easily be pounded into a white flour which has almost exactly the same nutrients as wheat flour. It even has gluten, so it can be made into a "springy" dough. On the running ends of these rhizomes are white sprouts that will be next year's cattails, and these make a remarkably palatable vegetable, eaten either raw or cooked. In the spring, when these sprouts have grown into fat young plants, they can be pulled from the rhizomes and the lower six or eight inches peeled to reveal a white heart that is so tender it can be pinched in two with the thumbnail. This is the "Cossack asparagus" I have mentioned, which tastes like cucumber eaten raw, and makes a mild-flavored cooked vegetable with considerable food value.

Later on, in May, cattail plants produce pencil-like bloom spikes. The upper or staminate part can be boiled and eaten as a very hearty, granular vegetable that nearly everyone likes. Then when the spikes become covered with pollen, you can walk through the marsh rubbing pollen off into a pail and gather several pounds an hour. It is as fine as the finest cake flour and makes some tasty high-protein pancakes.

The tules or bulrushes (*Scirpus acutus*) are just as good as the cattails, if not better. They, too, have large rhizomes ending in white sprouts in the winter, and these sprouts, too, can be cooked or eaten raw. They are juicy, crisp, and mild in flavor, slightly sweet and apparently quite nourishing. Even after they grow old, the bases of the plants can still be peeled and eaten. In Minnesota I once ate nothing for twenty-four hours but these bulrush bases—yet I still liked them the next day. Bulrush pollen can be collected and put on the menu the same way as cattail pollen. Ripe seeds of bulrush beaten off with a stick into a container make a very nutritious gruel when ground up, and can be made into bread or cakes.

The reeds (*Phragmites communis*) have other uses. I have heard that the roots are edible, but I find them far too woody and wiry to be attractive. Very young shoots, before they see the light of day, make a good cooked vegetable. In late spring or early summer, before the plants bloom, they are rich in starch and sugar. At this time the Indians gather great quantities of young plants, dry them in the hot desert sun until brittle, then pound the whole plant into a flour, sifting out the fibers. I know a farmer in New Mexico who dried and ground some of these sweet plants in his hammer mill, then sifted out the fibers. The remaining flour was self-rising and self-sweetened. Dampened, rolled into balls, and baked, they swelled up and were sweet as cookies. His children loved them. The large panicle of grain can also be harvested in the fall. It has a reddish hull very difficult to remove, but this never bothered the Indians. They ground it, hull and all, and made it into a gruel or mush that was not very appetizing in appearance, nor anything to write home about in flavor, but which did help keep body and soul together during those lean times.   We left the river valley and turned westward, toward Silver City, where one of my sons and his family live. Now we were in the arid grasslands, which is the part of the trip that would give me pause. However, I believe I could survive in this area nearly any time of the year—and in certain seasons I could grow fat.

Yucca and cactus, many species of both, grow in profusion. In August or early September, when both are in fruit, it would be a pleasure to walk across this country. The summer rains would have made the desert bloom, and the usually dry washes would have at least occasional pools of water. Many of the cacti, particularly prickly pear cacti, bear edible fruits. Even the seeds of these fruits can be roasted, ground, and eaten. When prickly pear is not in fruit, its flattened young stems—with the patches of stickers cut off—can be sliced and boiled to make a very good, if somewhat slimy, vegetable.

Yucca fruits can be eaten green as a vegetable or ripe as a sweet, nourishing fruit. My daughter-in-law served me both ripe and boiled green fruits of *Yucca baccata* that she had gathered and frozen, and they were delicious. Yucca will furnish food any time of the year. Indians in the region sharpen a stout pole to a chisel point on one end, drive this down inside the tough outside leaves, and pry the tender hearts from the plants. Next, they dig a trench, line it with stones, and build a fire in it to get the stones very hot. Then they remove the remains of the fire, line the pit with yucca leaves, drop the hearts on them, cover with more yucca leaves, and finally pile up a foot or so of dirt on top. All this is left until the next day, when one finds much sweet, nourishing food among the fibers of the yucca hearts. If the weather is cold—and these high deserts can get cold at night— one could sleep on top of the oven and have a wilderness equivalent of an electric blanket, then dig under the bed next morning for ready-cooked rations for the day!

Around Silver City there were many live oaks, piñons, and junipers on the hills. My grandchildren—who have long since caught the wild-food fever from me—had gathered many pounds of piñon nuts earlier in the fall. Last year there was a bumper crop of these exceedingly good nuts. All three grandchildren, two girls and a boy, have learned the Indian trick of feeding piñons into one corner of the mouth, shelling them by some dexterity of teeth and tongue, and allowing the shells to dribble from the other corner. Any one of them can eat a half-pound of these delicious nuts in half an hour.

The junipers bear oily berries which the Indians and Swedes eat, but which taste altogether too much like furniture polish for me to enjoy them. Maybe extreme hunger would enable me to tolerate that medicinal, aromatic flavor, but until the emergency becomes pretty dire the Indians and Swedes can have them. Live oaks, though, bear sweetish acorns that were valued by the Indians. They shelled them and ground the kernels into meal from which they leached excess tannin by percolating hot water through it before making a heavy, sticky bread that was very high in nourishment.

In most of the United States, purslane is a weed of cultivated ground, but out here it behaves like a real native. After the summer rains it comes up profusely among the sagebrush, and is so succulent and abundant that the range cattle use it for both food and drink, fattening so beautifully that they become almost as broad as they are long. This same weed is excellent food for man, eaten raw or cooked, fresh or dried. The seeds can be gathered by throwing a bunch of seeding plants on a sheet of plastic and letting them finish the job there. When ground, they make delicious "buckwheat cakes."

In the sparse brush and grasslands huge jackrabbits thrive. These would furnish endless quantities of meat to anyone who can aim a gun. Two of my son's neighbors get jackrabbits without guns. One has a lean, dark greyhound that can outrun them, and the other has a tame bobcat that can stalk them skillfully and then outrun them for short distances.

My son drove me across the Continental Divide, here just a barely perceptible ridge from which two gentle slopes carry the waters on the eastern side to the Atlantic and on the westward side toward the Pacific. We went on to the headwaters of the Gila River, which crosses southern Arizona, joining the Colorado at Yuma on the Arizona-California line.

If I ever have to make good my boast, I'll start at the mouth of the Rio Grande, in subtropical Brownsville, Texas, in very early spring. I'll then make my way leisurely up the Rio Grande Valley. Plant life along this valley, with the fish of the river and the small game I could snare along its edges, would keep me well fed. I would try to arrive in New Mexico, opposite the Gila, about the time the summer rains begin in July or August. Next would come the trek from river to river, living on yucca, cactus, purslane, jackrabbits, and any other desert food that presented itself. Then it would be down the Gila to Yuma, and down the Colorado to the Gulf of California. I'm afraid I'll never make that trip, but I can still dream—and it's fun to nibble about the edges of such a daring adventure.

9. Love-Out on an Island

ONE of my favorite places in the southern part of this country is Cumberland Island, the southernmost of the Sea Isles of Georgia, set right on the Georgia-Florida border. It is a good-sized mass of land, twenty miles long and several miles wide.

Cumberland is not a tourist resort—at least, not yet. The island has several owners, and they are under great pressure and great temptation to accept the unheard-of prices resort developers are willing to pay for this undeveloped primitive paradise. Right now, it's touch and go whether or not it will be preserved as a unique and irreplaceable wilderness habitat or turned into a multibillion-dollar resort of high-rise hotels and hotdog stands.

The bull alligator still bellows through the breeding season in the bayous of Cumberland Island. On its seaward side, a perfect sand beach stretches out of sight in both directions, usually without another person in view. Strange plants that flourish only on undisturbed semitropical southern shores find this island one of the last habitats in which they can thrive. I get a grand feeling of knowing that a bit of original southeastern wilderness remains intact to reveal to us what that part of our beautiful land was like before man ruined most of it. I also want my great-great-grandchildren to enjoy this same feeling. If Cumberland Island goes to the resort developers, something extremely precious will be lost to America, and by this loss every present and future American will be diminished.

One of the owners wants me to come down and identify the edible plants that grow wild on his island. He apparently knows what will lure me there. He sent up some grapefruit picked from its wild trees, and told me of the great beds of oysters, the succulent stone crabs, and the tidal streams full of shrimp from which I can take gourmet meals. I am very grateful for the privilege of spending a week on this island, a privilege that can be extended to very few without destroying that which makes it so wonderful to visit.

What do I expect to find there? Besides the crabs, shrimp, and oysters, I intend to look for other seafoods. Conch chowder is an excellent dish; and hot clam nectar, when made from tiny coquina clams which crowd these southern beaches, is a beverage for the gods.

But I expect to spend most of my time exploring the strange plant life of this island. Besides the wild grapefruit which I have already tasted and approved, I expect to find wild limes and wild bitter oranges. These wild oranges are nothing to shout about as fresh fruit or juice, but they make the best orange marmalade ever tasted. I hope to can a supply while there.

There will be palm hearts, crudely called "palm cabbage" by some insensitive souls. Comparing this delicacy to cabbage is like comparing lobster to salt codfish. I have not tasted fresh palm heart since 1963, when I gathered some where the trees had been cut to make a parking lot in Louisiana. I get very hungry thinking of a salad of stone crab claw and a few small chunks of garden-ripened fresh pineapple. This is the *Sabal palmetto*, and its smaller relative, *Sabal etonia*, or scrub palmetto. Both these plants also bear fruits with very scanty, prunelike pulp once relished by the Indians.

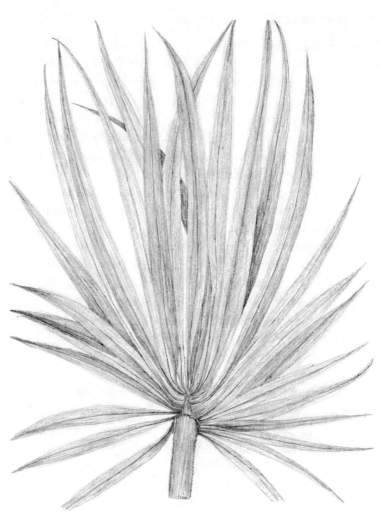

Sabal palmetto.

And this time I'm going to try the saw palmetto (*Serenoa repens*), which has a reputation for producing a very small, tedious-to-gather palm heart, but the best-flavored one of them all. This little palm also produces fruit relished by the Indians, but the only description of it I can find doesn't exactly fill me with enthusiasm. A visitor to the Indians in 1699, speaking of this same palmetto, said, "They gave us some of the berries to eat; we tasted them, but not one among us could suffer them to stay in our mouths, for we could compare the taste of them to nothing else but rotten cheese steeped in tobacco juice." Not a great recommendation for this fruit—but another record says that early settlers in Florida mixed the juice of the palmetto berries with carbonated water, and the beverage had a good sale, so maybe there are ways to make it palatable.

I expect to meet some old friends, too, or at least some relatives of old friends. Along the fifty or more miles of saltwater shores there will be the southern species of the orach, glasswort, sea rocket, seablite, and sea purslane—all offering excellent materials for salads and many a good dish of cooked greens. They'll know how to cook them down there, with a piece of hog jowl for seasoning, and some pepper sauce and cornbread to go with them. I expect to find poke, the same kind that grows in my backyard. There are grapes in southeastern Georgia that sometimes get mixed up about the seasons in the warm climate and bear a crop of fruit in the wintertime. Some plants grow *only* in the winter down there.

Remember the "bull-nettle," "spurge nettle," "tread-softly," or "malo-jujer" plant? It has nutlike seeds, and a friend sent me some. I find a report that a species of this plant, *Cnidoscolus stimulosa*, grows on sand dunes on Cumberland. Now I discover that this plant not only has an edible seed, but deep under the sand produces a fine potato-like tuber that is said to be both palatable and nutritious. I'm going to make up for my previous neglect of this plant by giving it much attention during my week there, if it is visible at this season.

I expect to find several species of the prickly pear cactus on the island. I doubt that I will find any edible fruit so early in the spring, but the young, tender stems—called "leaves" by most amateurs—will make an exceedingly palatable vegetable if the clusters of stickers are cut away with a sharp knife. There are several kinds of fruit-bearing cacti on the island, on which I wish I could spend a year, sampling everything in its own season.

I want to experiment further with some of the cat briers of the

South. *Smilax bona-nox* and *S. havanensis* should both be found
there. The first one is called "bull-brier," "Chinabrier," "blas-
pheme vine," or "stretch-berry," depending on where it grows.
Get caught only once in its thick tangle of fierce briers and you
will have a sudden revelation about how it got the name "blas-
pheme vine." When I was a child, we used to chew two or three
of the rubbery berries with some sweet gum, the fragrant exuda-
tion of the liquid amber tree. The smilax berries made the gum
stretchier and noisier—and why else does a child chew gum?

Though chewing gum no longer fascinates me, other parts of
the smilax vine do. The young shoots should be about right
when I arrive, in April, and I love them both cooked and raw.
Raw, I either eat them right in the woods, or chop them into a
salad. Cooked, I eat them somewhat like a cold asparagus salad,
chilled and liberally smeared with mayonnaise. The Indians
cooked the tuberous roots when young and tender and ate them
like potatoes. When older and tougher, the roots were chopped
fine, beaten in mortars, and the reddish starch washed out in
cold water and allowed to settle. The water was poured off, and
the starchy meal dried. This meal was sometimes mixed with
cornmeal to make cakes fried in bear grease, which were considered a great delicacy. Or it was sweetened with wild honey and
boiled with water, and when cooled it became a highly prized
jelly. I have tried that pounding and it is brutally hard work. This
time I'm going to try chopping the roots with water in an electric
blender, and see if that isn't easier. I find an electric blender so
handy in preparing primitive foods that I often wonder how
Indians got by without this versatile gadget!

I expect to find much that will be strange to me, but I won't
feel a stranger, for everywhere among the flora I expect to sight
old friends, some that I have not seen since my Southern boy-
hood. I know that even the strange plants and I will get along,
for I will accept them on their own terms—not on the terms that
people apply to them. Thus I am likely to love what other people
call pests. The water hyacinth, which is condemned for clogging

southern waterways, is a beautiful flower. The young leaves, leaf stalks, and flower bud clusters all make delicious vegetables when thoroughly boiled, seasoned, and eaten with pepper sauce and hot buttered corn pone. And the coarse sawgrass that covers swamps and marshes—both fresh and brackish—with its sharp-edged leaves as tall as a man, if carefully pulled and peeled at the base, yields a tender little "palm heart" about three inches long that is very tasty either raw or cooked.

The only thing bothering me is that I wonder if I will ever be able to enjoy that island as much in the realization as I already have in anticipation!

10. Interlude on
an Unspoiled Island

WARM islands, swaying palms, and wild pigs are the stuff that dreams are made of. Cumberland Island is not in the tropics, but it is far enough south so that huge alligators haunt its freshwater sloughs; wild pigs, wild cattle, and wild horses roam its woods and feed in the salt marshes. A freshwater lake and stream are alive with fish, and in the tidal creeks are enough oysters to give every reader of this book a generous oyster dinner without endangering the supply. There are also unlimited clams, crabs, and saltwater fishes of many kinds in these same tidal streams.

Did you ever drive from winter into summer in one day? We left Pennsylvania as a cold storm was threatening, one that we later learned dropped thirteen inches of snow on Easter Sunday. A few white flakes were falling as we pulled out of the driveway, but by the time we had passed Baltimore it had turned to a warm drizzle. Just south of Washington, D.C., we saw our first daffodil in bloom. Another hour, and forsythia yellowed the landscape. Before lunch we were already seeing riotously blooming azaleas

68

of many colors, flowering cherries, and orchards massed with bloom in which bees were at work collecting honey and pollinating this year's crop of fruit. Then we reached an area where all daffodils were long since gone, and the forsythia was looking ragged and finished, and even the azaleas were well past their prime. We stopped every hour or so to shed more clothes; by nightfall we were looking for a motel that had air conditioning and rubbing our reddened arms and faces with suntan lotion.

An island is a small body of land surrounded by the need for a boat, and our hosts met us in a beautiful craft that made getting there half the fun. It was low tide, and the extensive salt marshes on the landward side of Cumberland were dotted with the resident wild horses, cattle, and pigs, out stuffing themselves on the lush growth of the semi-aquatic habitat. We jeeped from the dock to the house on a sand road that wound through palmettos and longleaf yellow pines.

The grounds around the Southern mansion were picturesque with palms and live oaks draped in Spanish moss. I wanted to see the vegetable garden. There is something very alluring about an area where one can just keep gardening regardless of season —and have your own fresh, vitamin-filled vegetables the year around. The soil had originally been quite sandy, but it has been built up with organic methods—mainly mulch and manure—until it is a deep, black, easily worked loam. My host said gardening here is mainly a matter of dropping seed in the ground, then stepping back quickly so the growing plant won't hit you in the face.

By making successive plantings they enjoy collards, turnips and turnip greens, mustard greens, radishes, onions, lettuce, peas, and many other vegetables throughout the winter. As summer approaches, these cool-weather plants are gradually replaced by such heat-lovers as tomatoes, sweet corn, green beans, and black-eyed peas. As each planting comes into bearing, older plantings are abandoned, allowed to make a good growth, then turned under as green manure. The garden is huge, allowing plenty of room for such practices, and there is always a vacant spot or two for planting any vegetable that strikes one's fancy. If the weather gets dry, there is a flowing artesian well ready to furnish all the irrigation water needed.

We feasted on "soul food"—turnip greens cooked with hog jowl, sausage made of venison and pork, combined according to a recipe furnished by Lyndon Johnson which starts off: "Take one deer and one hog . . ." Both the hog and the deer were native products. With the meal we had corn pone hot from the oven.

I unpacked my fishing gear and walked out to a little pond near the house. After chasing a three-foot alligator from the dam I took his place and began casting for both bass and bream, landing a fish with almost every cast. The bream—which they pronounce "brim"—is the same fish we call bluegill in Pennsylvania. But the ones I catch back home range from five to seven inches long, while these were from eight to ten inches long and averaged about a pound apiece. My hosts said they thought them too bony, but when I demonstrated how easily one could fillet the meat and get two beautiful little boneless fillets, they enthusiastically learned this technique. So for breakfast we had more soul food, fish and grits. The bream were declared the sweetest fish ever tasted, once the bothersome bones were gone. Hominy grits make the perfect accompaniment for this fish.

Our hosts and other guests insisted that I prepare an authentic Hawaiian luau, such as I describe in my *Beachcomber's Handbook*. I agreed—with the condition that it be all wild food and that everyone help gather it. At any luau the *pièce de résistance* is a pig roasted in an underground oven called an *imu*. You don't *hunt* wild pigs on Cumberland Island. The pigs are so plentiful and have become so used to jeeps that you merely drive around and select one. Two others went after the meat while the rest of us prepared the *imu*.

We dug a hole in the ground, built a fire in it and another fire beside it. Then we struck our first snag. An *imu* needs rocks to heat—and Cumberland Island has no rocks. We finally found a pile of bricks that would serve. Some of the bricks were thrown into the fire at the bottom of the hole and the others into the fire beside it. Leaving one person to feed the fires, we set off for more food.

On the ocean side of Cumberland there is a wide, white-sand beach stretching for twenty miles without a soul on it. It is as smooth as Daytona Beach, and we skimmed along it in a jeep. I finally persuaded the driver that we were not in the Daytona races and got him to drive close to the dunes on the upper beach and to slow down enough so I could spot any edible plants. They soon appeared—young, tender sea rocket, a member of the mustard family, with fleshy leaves that somewhat resemble mustard greens but with a horseradish tang, plus sea blite and orach growing in the windrow of debris at high-water line. While gathering these I found something I had not expected this far north: coconuts. Coconuts don't grow on Cumberland, but the sea carries them from the Bahamas, and they littered the upper beaches in places. Most were not good, but some sloshed when shaken, a sure sign that they were still edible.

When we returned with our plunder, we found that the others had not been idle. One fellow had taken a boat into the tidal stream and had brought back a great bunch of mullet, caught in a cast-net, a technique shared by Hawaiians and Cumberland Islanders. They also had several dozen blue crabs, a bag of clams, and another of oysters.

We made up a Cumberland Island version of the Hawaiian *laulau*. I filleted the mullet and then diced it, added onions and—because we had no taro tops—mixed in the beach greens, blite, rocket, and orach. We had no *ti* leaves to wrap it in, so we used squares of aluminum foil and made two dozen packages of the mixture. Hawaiians don't use clams and oysters with their luaus, but they do eat a sort of shellfish called an *opihi*, a kind of limpet, so I figured clams and oysters could substitute. They were shucked, then ground, mixed with bread crumbs, onion and other seasonings, then packed back into the clam shells, wrapped in foil and pronounced ready for the oven.

The oven was ready for them, too, and for all the rest of the food. The pig was white and beautifully cleaned. We covered the fire in the pit with a layer of palmetto leaves, then placed the pig in a cradle of chicken wire, so we could lift him out later without the meat coming apart, and lowered him into the pit. Around the pig we packed the laulaus and stuffed clams. Next we added another layer of leaves, then all the rest of the hot bricks, filled the pit with dirt, and left it for five hours.

Meanwhile we made a salad from the meat of the crabs, thinly sliced palm heart, and pineapple. The coconuts were opened and the meat grated, then covered with boiling water and the cream squeezed out through a strainer. This is sweetened, thickened with cornstarch, and boiled, then cooled until it jells, and cut into cubes. This is called *haupia* in Hawaiian and it makes the perfect dessert for a luau.

After the five hours had passed and everyone was getting weak with hunger, we finally opened the *imu*, to be greeted by one of the most appetizing aromas I ever sniffed. How everyone ate! One would have thought we were a herd of wild pigs. Everything, from the first aroma of the roasted pig to the *haupia*, was appreciated.

One might think the rest of our stay would have been anticlimactic, but not so. The island afforded endless diversion for a naturalist and gourmet, with its fascinating life forms and matchless foods. One day we had an oyster roast, a great way to combine fun and food. Another day our host flew five of us in his plane over Okefenokee Swamp. My heart was gladdened to see that every little island in the deep swamp had one or more alligators sunning on it. The alligator is still far from extinct in this area, but we must totally outlaw the use of alligator leather or they will not last much longer. Coming back over Cumberland we saw that that, too, was far from destitute of alligators.

Flying low on our return over the freshwater sloughs of Cumberland itself, we saw at least a dozen ten-foot 'gators sunning themselves in the sand.

After a week of such joys, we sadly said goodbye to some of the most gracious hosts I have ever visited. Southern hospitality is more than a legend. We got back to Pennsylvania in time to see the last of the Easter snow, but still in plenty of time to gather the first dandelion greens that dared to show their heads above the cold earth. Now, a few weeks later, our area is riotous with spring, and I wouldn't trade it for the whole Southland— but I'm already looking forward to my next visit to that wonderful section of America.

11. Survival in the Wilds of Central Park

ONE fall a reporter from New York called me and asked if he could do a story on me. I have learned to be cautious about such interviews, since many interviewers want to portray me as some kind of weed-eating freak, like the man in the carnival sideshow who eats beer glasses and swallows razor blades. I agreed to cooperate only if the writer would spend a day with me out in the fields, woods, and stream valleys, foraging materials for a wild party, and then share the meal with me. I'm sure he thought I would have him browsing directly from the trees, but he was a courageous soul and agreed to my conditions.

We spent several hours walking through woods and fields and wading stream beds, all the while collecting great quantities of wild foods. Then I spent several more hours in my kitchen cooking what we had collected. I also added a few wild delicacies that I had gathered at other seasons and stored in my freezer.

I know that people are expecting me to feed them fare that is not only rough and coarse, but so wild it has to be tied to the table to keep it from running away. So I delight in preparing these wild dishes in as civilized a manner as possible and serving them attractively. On this day I started the meal with a wild cherry soup served in beautiful lacquer bowls, with a gob of sour cream (which did not come from a wild cow) floating on top of each serving. After that we had a crayfish cocktail that is better than anyone's shrimp. The main dish was tenderloin of venison cooked in a coconut cream sauce. With it we had cattail bloom spikes, a very palatable vegetable with a granular texture, cooked like asparagus spears and served in a glass carafe filled with hot, salted water on which melted butter floated. This was on a candle trivet to keep the bloom buds piping hot. As each pencil-like spike was lifted from the carafe it was salted and buttered to perfection. For a second vegetable we had milkweed buds, prepared by a process that debitterizes them, leaving them tasting like an unusually good broccoli.

The salad was a dream concocted from the leafy tips of tender purslane, the sour leaves of sorrel, the slightly pungent wild watercress, tangy wild mint, halved ground cherries (like tiny, yellow wild tomatoes), thin crisp slices of snow-white Jerusalem artichoke tubers, and finally wild black walnut meats sprinkled over all. There was even a hint of wild garlic in the dressing.

Bread was made of a persimmon–hickory-nut mixture that I find absolutely delicious, and was served with a wide choice of wild-fruit jams and jellies. Beverages were dandelion wine and wild-chicory coffee, while for dessert we had May apple chiffon pie. Of course the May apple is not an apple, but a lemonlike wild fruit of the barberry family. As we were sipping our wild-grape aperitifs and nibbling on bits of candied wild calamus heart, the reporter admitted that he was surprised.

However, he was surprised more by the lush countryside around my Pennsylvania farmhouse than he was by my performance. He insisted that if I were removed from our Garden of Eden, I would have a tough time preparing such a meal. I pointed out that I had once lived a week on a Maine island on

nothing but wild foods and had enjoyed a continuous feast, and
had prepared complete wild meals in such widely scattered local-
ities as Indiana, New Mexico, Washington State, Hawaii, Quebec, and New Jersey. He readily admitted that perhaps several
fruitful spots existed where I could do this sort of thing, but he
still had a suspicion that I must pick my spot carefully before I
could collect enough of these dainty wild tidbits to make a really
good meal. "I could gather enough wild food in Central Park,
right in the heart of New York City, to make a good meal," I
told him, finally.

His only answer was a noncommital "Hmm" and a long, con-
templative look. I should have known that look spelled trouble.
When the reporter returned to New York, he talked to an editor,
and then my phone rang. He challenged me to make good my
boast by gathering enough wild food from Central Park for a
meal I would cook and then eat.

I agreed to give it a try, and the editor sent along a photographer to see that I didn't cheat.

We entered the park at West 86th Street and hardly had
stepped off the traverse road when I saw some young and tender
lamb's quarters coming up where something had disturbed an
area of earth. This was a find indeed, for, although lamb's quarters is probably the most common weed in New York, even
springing up between the cracks of sidewalks, it is usually found
in its edible stage in late spring. However, if the earth is turned
or disturbed in late summer, a new fall crop will shoot up. This
plant is closely related to garden spinach and makes a good
spinachy-type food when well cooked. I began pinching off the
leafy tops and stuffing a plastic bag.

All about me I could see plants that would offer food at other
seasons. In early spring that great patch of Japanese knotweed,
or "false bamboo," as it is sometimes called, sticks up tender
little sprouts that look like asparagus and taste like rhubarb. But
they were all old now, tough and inedible. Mulberry trees over-
hung every path, but their fruit had long ago been claimed by

Curly Dock.

boys and squirrels. Two kinds of wild cherries were abundant but long since past the season of fruiting.

Then I spied the beautiful purple stems of an old poke, or inkberry plant. In the spring, poke has good fat sprouts that rival asparagus, but in the fall the old plant is not only inedible but actually poisonous after it develops the purple dye that makes its old stems so attractive. But the poke wasn't a total loss. The birds had eaten the purple-black berries and had scattered the seeds all around, so little six-inch poke seedlings were coming up under every bush, and young seedlings are edible any time of the year you can find them. I filled another plastic bag.

In this same area I also found curly dock (*Rumex crispus*) putting on new growth in the warm, fall weather. The old, summer-grown leaves would be too tough and bitter to eat, but the cool-weather-grown little leaves in the center of each plant were sweet and mild. Another bag came into use. In a neglected flower bed I spied the clover-like leaves of sour grass, a good salad plant that makes vinegar or lemon juice unnecessary. Nearby was a sturdy growth of peppergrass (*Lepidium virginicum*) with its green seed pods, called "poor man's pepper," which make a tasty, pungent salad material. A few minutes later I discovered a great patch of wild onions (*Allium vineale*), a welcome find as the green tops or crushed bulbs will cure any salad of the banality with which altogether too many of them are afflicted. Out came another bag.

Food was accumulating, but my lunch still had an awfully greenish cast. I badly wanted a not-so-green something with which to pad it out. I didn't have access to that freezerful of wild goodies on which I depend at home, and I was feeling the pinch.

The park was almost filled with oaks, hickories, butternuts, and black walnuts, and the nuts of any of them would have been a welcome addition to that green lunch, but the squirrels had already eaten them all and all I could find were empty shells.

Those squirrels? I have eaten a Brunswick stew made of squirrel meat and thought it very fine fare indeed. No! Impossible. Get thee behind me, Satan! I haven't the heart to kill a truly wild creature, let alone these gentle squirrels that clustered about my feet, trustingly begging me for food. Even the venison I served to the feature writer was a present from a hunter friend, for I find the gut-wringing aches of conscience that come when I try to shoot an innocent creature too high a price to pay for a little meat. I would as soon kill the photographer, who was questioning the "wildness" of everything I picked, as injure one of these trusting little squirrels. In fact, I'd rather.

How about those pigeons strutting on the walk? Weren't they considered a nuisance, and didn't I have a civic duty? A pigeon pot-pie is a dish not to be lightly passed by, and a fat pigeon stuffed with celery and bacon and roasted in a wrapping of wild grape leaves is a gourmet's delight. But no, again. Same objections, same reasons. If these beautiful birds must be destroyed, someone else will have to do the dirty work. I turned my back on them and walked down into the grassy glade near the lake.

Despite the Park Department's care(?), the dandelions were competing very successfully with the grass. Some of them had apparently mistaken the Indian summer for spring, and were putting on a new crop of flowers. Most people who eat dandelions are under the mistaken impressions that the "greens" or leaves are the only edible part, and think that they can be eaten only in very early spring. But I have discovered that in the fall, after a few freezes, the dandelion becomes sweet and good again. And I have also discovered that the upper part of the white root, and the white stem or crown that reaches from the top of the root to the surface of the ground, are much better flavored than the leaves, and, best of all for today, this part of the dandelion is white, not green. I was liking my lunch a little better.

By a stroke of sheer good luck, the dandelions also helped to solve my main-dish problem. As I was shoving my knife into the ground and cutting off the plants at the roots, a small boy carrying two paper cups came to watch me. He must have guessed that I wanted the weeds for food, for he finally came up and said, in a sympathetic voice, "Mister, you must be awfully hungry. Would you like to have these fish?" The two paper cups were filled with little three-inch sunfish he had caught by seining the lake edge with a perforated plastic bag. The poor things were nearly dead, but still flopping. The kind thing to do was to accept them gratefully, then kill them as quickly and humanely as possible. That's what I did.

Things were looking up. I wouldn't go lunchless this day. Then I found a small thicket of sassafras—and remembered that I would need a beverage with all that food. I love sassafras tea, but I am not a vandal who goes around indiscriminately pulling out plants. Indeed, my morning's work had helped the city in the task of weeding Central Park. Now how was I to get sassafras roots without doing damage? Suddenly it occurred to me that where one sassafras sprout is pulled, two usually grow back. And I also remembered that the chief trouble with this shrub, as an ornamental, is that it tends to grow too thickly. These rationalizations eased my conscience, and I soon had a plastic bag full of the fragrant roots.

Next I found a wild crabapple tree with some ripe fruit still hanging on it. These crabapples are tiny, hard, and sour, but thinly sliced they will add a tang to a tossed salad that can't be achieved with any other material. I was ready to head for the kitchen.

The first task on reaching the reporter's apartment was to clean this mess of wildings of city dust and grime. Everything had to be washed, rewashed, and then washed again and again.

Then came the paring, peeling, and preparation. The dandelions furnished the hardest job. Each plant had to be inverted, and all the dark-colored root material carefully pared away from the base with a sharp knife. Then the older, outside leaves were pulled away and discarded, leaving only the tender heart of each plant. The tiny, newly born leaves in the center of each plant, plus the little white buds down among the leaf-stems that had intended to grow into flowers were both carefully removed and saved, for these are salad material *par excellence*. Green parts of other leaves were trimmed off and rejected, leaving only a tender white crown from each plant that is utterly delicious when properly cooked. The green leaves are perfectly edible, but this time of year they are a little tough, and I had such a wealth of food that I could afford to throw them away.

The potherbs'—lamb's quarters, poke, and dock—larger stems were removed, then they were cooked together in one superbly blended dish of greens. The salad materials—sour grass, wild onion, peppergrass, crabapples, plus young leaves and unborn buds of dandelions—were given a couple of extra washings, then chopped into a tossed salad that was strictly an original. The sassafras roots were not only washed, but scrubbed, then cut in short pieces and boiled in a huge kettle of water— perfuming the kitchen with a spicy fragrance. The little fish were beheaded and skinned, and the fins cut away. Then each was dipped in a tempura batter and fried to a golden brown.

By careful timing, all this cooking was concluded at the same time, and my lunch was soon on the table. How did it taste? Well, I hate to go into superlatives about my own creations, so let's just say that it was eminently edible. The dandelion crowns, scalded by several dunkings in boiling water, then steamed until they were tender, tasted like artichoke hearts—only more so. The greens? Well, spinach never tasted *that* good. Each little fish, the freshest ever served in New York, was a morsel of savory goodness, mild and very unfishy. The wild salad made all tame tossed salads pale into insignificance. And that sassafras tea!

By now a small group had collected in the reporter's kitchen to watch this wild operation, and, while we had not collected enough food to invite them all to lunch, we could offer every-body a steaming cup of sassafras tea. They were unanimous in its praise.

By this time I was really hungry, but before I was through, fork-bearers came from all directions, asking a taste. I managed to get a few bites of everything before the plate was emptied. I sat there, still hungry, wondering what was growing up in Fort Tryon Park, around the Cloisters, that I could gather and eat!

12. The Best Food in Town

ONE late autumn Saturday I was teaching a class on wild-food gathering and cooking at Kitchiwan Research Station of Brooklyn Botanic Garden, in New York City. It is located in a rural area on the Taconic Parkway, but most of my students were from New York City. They were delighted to find how many wild delicacies were nearby, and were genuinely enthusiastic over the lunch we prepared. However, they all mentioned that because they lived in the city, nature could never continue to be enjoyed this way.

Finally, I told them that even New York City had more nature in it than a man could learn about in a lifetime of study. I said *I* had once gathered enough wild food for a meal from Central Park. They challenged me. This was Saturday. Could I, with no prior exploration or preparation, and avoiding Central Park, which I had already explored, find enough food for a really decent dinner and actually cook and eat that dinner?

A Bucknell student named Jim was with me as a helper. We

consulted and decided to accept the challenge. Next morning, as we crossed the Harlem River, we sharpened our foraging eyes and began looking for likely places to gather food.

At 150th Street, between the West Side Highway and the Hudson River, there is an athletic field and a park of sorts. Hawthorn trees loaded with ripe fruit beckoned, so we pulled off the road and parked. But there are haws and haws, and these were hard and bitter, so we left them on the trees. However, there was an undeveloped section of the park at the south end, a weed-grown, untended lot, just the kind of place where wild food abounds. A wild grapevine ran over tall sumac bushes. We took some of the small grapes and also some sumac heads to make a lemonade-like drink. Lamb's quarters were plentiful— and only the day before one of my students had told me of experimenting with this weed while it was bearing unripe seeds. Not only did it turn out to be a good cooked vegetable, he said, but it was a much heartier dish than the young lamb's quarters, which closely resembles spinach. We filled a plastic bag with the fruiting parts.

There were also fat dandelion plants, and these are as good after a few frosts as they are in the spring. We loaded another bag, and were ready to move on, when Jim called my attention to a shaggy-mane mushroom, one of the very finest of the wild mushrooms, in the prime of readiness. With our eyes opened, we soon found that there were hundreds, if not thousands, of these hiding in the weeds. Here was a find indeed. Our dinner was beginning to look good.

Through a hole in the fence we crawled, and out on the green next to the river. Right down by the river's edge we found first-year evening primroses growing far too thickly for their own good, so we liberated a few of them. These wild flowers produce a rosette of leaves and large carrotlike pink roots the first year, which are mildly pungent when properly cooked and seasoned. Here also grew orach, a plant usually found on saltwater shores, but doing fine here on this tidal water that is mostly fresh, and

Evening Primrose.   Orach.

useful as a cooked vegetable or for salad. Everywhere, there was green-seeded peppergrass, not a grass at all, but a member of the mustard family. The tasty green seeds would contribute to the salad we planned, as would a few bulbs of the wild garlic that seems to grow wherever anyone tries to raise a lawn.

After this, we drove to Brooklyn's Prospect Park. While digging dandelions I had come on some fine earthworms. We had a couple of fishing rods in the station wagon, and I wanted to try for a main dish in the park lake. After two hours of casting, still-fishing, bottom-fishing, and top-fishing, I still could not tell anyone the best way to catch fish in that city lake. Somehow, I caught two little eight-inch perch. Jim had long since deserted me and wandered up the stream that fed the lake, carrying my landing net. He returned with two bullfrogs he had netted, plus a quantity of cattail sprouts, the tender little white horns that had intended to be next year's cattails.

On the way back to the parking lot, we came on a hawthorn

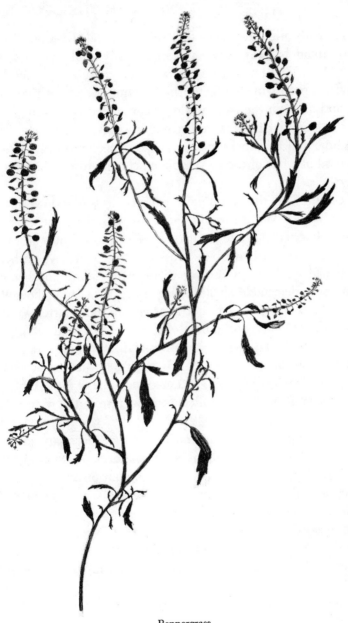

Peppergrass.

loaded with bright-red haws that were soft and sweet and had a flavor about halfway between a ripe, mealy apple and a strawberry. We filled our plastic bag with dessert. On a nearby hill, sassafras sprouts made a little thicket. Jim was afraid that pulling up bushes in the park would be considered vandalism, but I pointed out that these were becoming weeds, threatening other planting, and that maintenance people would probably be glad to be rid of a few of them. We pulled enough to furnish us with tea.

According to the morning paper, it was about low tide at Coney Island. We drove out there and found the beach completely deserted this late in the year. The lower stones of a rock jetty were covered with blue mussels. We could have gathered a ton had we had any use for them. After filling another bag with these delectable shellfish, we drove to a store, bought a couple of eggs and a small bottle of cream, then started looking for a place to fix our dinner. Near the east end of Coney Island (which has not been an island for many years) we found a bluff above the beach. By setting up our dinner camp just at the base of this bluff, we could see none of New York but had a magnificent view of rollers coming in from the wide Atlantic.

Several trips between car and beach were necessary to carry the camp stove, cooking utensils, icebox loaded with wild food, fuel and water containers. (Jim is a sanitation nut, so he dissolved a number of chlorine tablets in the water in which he washed the salad materials, despite my argument that New York water needed more chlorine like ocean water needed more salt.) We peeled away the dandelions until only the tender center leaves were left, then minced them finely with the peppergrass and wild garlic. The orach was left in larger pieces, while the cattail sprouts were cut into little white disks. All this was tossed with a little salt and some salad oil.

I washed the wild grapes, cooked them until they popped open and the juice was flowing, then strained out the seeds and

skins, sweetened the juice just enough to make a sweet-tart concoction—and returned this liquid to the stove to pour in a flour
paste for thickening. Next, I boiled this fruit soup until it was
slightly thickened and had a clearish look. This became our ap-
petizer.

Then I made the sumac-ade. We had a supply of hard red
berries with an acid coating from a plant botanists call *Rhus
glabra.* Our students the day before had christened the beverage
made from it "rhus-jhus." The red berries were simply stirred in
cold water until the water tasted as sour as if one had added
several lemons to it. At the same time it became a light pink
color, like circus lemonade. I strained it through a cloth and
sweetened it to taste—again not too sweet, for this was to be our
dry wine to go with our fish main dishes.

The primrose roots, scraped and sliced into little disks, were
cooked until tender, then salted and seasoned with a spoonful of
salad oil. The green-seeded lamb's quarters was cooked through
two waters to give it a milder flavor, then seasoned the same
way. Health-conscious Jim asked if I weren't destroying some of
the vitamins with all that cooking. I admitted that I might be
destroying about half, but since lamb's quarters has about four
times as much vitamin A and C as most domestic vegetables, it
still would be about twice as nutritious as our usual fare.

The little fish and the frog legs were skinned, then floured and
grilled whole. The mussels were steamed until open and firm-
fleshed, then arranged on the half-shell and covered with a roux
made of mussel broth, egg yolks, and cream. We carefully
washed the mushrooms with a damp cloth to remove the outer
scale, leaving them a sinless white. These were diced roughly
and sautéed, the juice, thickened with a little flour, served over
them.

Sassafras roots were scrubbed clean, then boiled until the
water turned a pleasing reddish color and was delightfully fragrant. The haws were wastefully sliced to discard the seedy center sections. (Why be picayune with food that is so abundantly

free?) The bowls of haw slices were covered with slightly sweetened heavy cream.

I doubt that anyone in New York dined better than Jim and I did that evening.

After our magnificent dinner I took out a notebook and began totting up the bill. Two eggs, a small carton of cream, and some raw sugar, oil and flour from the camp supplies—it all came to less than one dollar. Jim ungraciously remarked that had we worked as hard at our regular jobs we could easily have earned enough money to buy the finest meal in New York and had it served by a tuxedoed waiter. But I rejected this argument. We had not worked, we had played—very hard but very enjoyably—all day, and I doubted that anyone else had more fun than we did in New York's parks that Sunday. Besides, the excellent dinner we had just consumed had a meaning no purchased dinner could ever achieve. It was a symbol of our intimacy and creative fellowship with nature, and proof that such a relationship could be experienced even in New York City.

*Stalking
the
Wild Et Cetera*

Mountain Maple.

Striped Maple.

Sugar Maple.

Norway Maple.

Red Maple.

Silver Maple.

Box Elder.

13. Tree Saps—
Barrels of Sweet Fun

YOU don't have to live where the snow gets neck deep to a giraffe in order to enjoy the pleasure of making your own maple syrup. Perfectly good maple syrup and maple sugar can be made in South Carolina, Tennessee, Arkansas, Oklahoma, and even northern Texas, as well as in all the states north and west of these locations. You don't even need sugar maples. Many other maples know the same trick. Of course, Dixieland is not likely to challenge Vermont in producing maple syrup commercially. But if you want to make some of this finest of sweets as a hobby there are many more places in this country where it can be done than places where it can't.

A few years ago I started swinging a wild brace-and-bit through the woodlands of several states, and made some very interesting discoveries. Given free run of a wooded campus in southern Pennsylvania, I just let myself go. I consulted a Canadian student about techniques and was solemnly assured by him that it would be impossible to make sugar in our local climate as the weather was too warm and the maple trees too far advanced by sugaring time. It apparently hadn't occurred to him that this might merely indicate that sugaring time would be earlier in this climate. I convinced him that we should experiment, and on the first warm day of late winter, about two months before sugaring time in his Quebec home, we tapped a few sugar maples and found them flowing copiously, much to my friend's amazement.

When I began tapping Norway maples, silver maples, red maples, and even box elders, my Canadian friend at first thought I couldn't tell one tree from another. When I assured him that I knew what I was doing, but wanted to see what these trees had to offer, he thought I had taken leave of my senses. Even when I pointed out that these trees seemed to be yielding large amounts of sap that tasted just as sweet as that from the sugar maples, he still shook his head and disapproved. He finally withdrew from the project because he thought I had no respect for tradition. He was right. I don't.

How about this climate clog? My experience indicates that it is weather that is important, not climate. When nights are frosty and days warm, the sap will flow, and all states north of Florida have at least a few days of such weather between Christmas and Easter. When a warm spell arrived during the January thaw, I tapped the trees, much to the horror of all knowledgeable sugarmakers. The fine weather held for a week, and by the time the deep freeze descended again I had seven gallons of freshly made maple syrup, a pure bonus, for the same trees flowed again six weeks later. A single warm, frostless night will not stop the flow. Indeed, you are likely to find all the sap buckets overflowing the next morning, and the trees still gushing. A prolonged warm spell will gradually dry up the run and bring the season to an end.

How much equipment do you need to indulge in this hobby? Partly because I had little money, and partly because I always have objected to spending more than a resulting product is worth, I kept my equipment simple, even primitive. The spiles, or spigots, I made from four-inch sections of elderberry or sumac stems, pushing out the soft pith with an iron rod, sharpening one end so I could drive it into the hole I'd drilled in the tree, then cutting a notch on which to hang the sap bucket.

"Sap bucket" is a pretty fancy name for the tin cans and fruit jars to which I attached wire bails. I made evaporators from two large bake pans the school kitchen was discarding. Most people have a brace-and-bit about the place and can find a milk can, washtub, or some other large container for sap storage. And that about completes the equipment that you actually need, in my opinion. A Vermonter would laugh loud and long at my operation, but I would laugh right back. When he makes maple syrup, he's working. When I make it, I'm playing.

Tap the tree by drilling a five-eighth-inch hole on the sunny side of the tree, as low as you can get it and still have plenty of room for your sap can to hang. The heartwood yields no sap, so it is useless to drill a deep hole; two inches is plenty. As soon as you remove the bit, you will see the edges of the hole getting damp. Drive in your spigot, hang your sap can over it, then watch it drip. Collecting sap is not nearly as tedious an operation as I expected it to be. I have seen a red maple not more than eight inches in diameter drip one or two gallons per day throughout the season. I once collected fourteen gallons of sap from a Norway maple in twenty-four hours during a warm-night flow.

The tedious part is evaporating; it takes 40 gallons of the sap to make one gallon of syrup of the proper consistency; that's a lot of water to boil away. Don't try to make more than a pint or so of maple syrup on your kitchen stove. I once initiated a young friend into the mysteries of mapling. He tapped the maples in his yard and insisted, against my advice, on evaporating enough sap in his mother's kitchen to make two gallons of syrup. When eighty gallons of water were released as steam inside the house, the wallpaper began peeling away from the walls, the draperies and furniture got soggy—and his mother still refuses to speak to me.

Wherever there are maples to tap, there will be fallen

branches and other dead wood about. I collected a few rocks and laid together a very crude fireplace, over which I leveled my bake pans. I built a fire under them. Boiling the sap over a campfire doubles the fun. When reduced about four to one, the sap is already pleasantly sweet. I dug some sassafras roots from under a nearby bush, washed them in the stream, chopped them into short pieces, and boiled them with some of this sweet juice in a sap can. That way, I had a warming refreshment as I worked.

With this primitive rig I easily evaporated forty gallons of sap to make one gallon of syrup a day. Deep pots make very poor evaporators. Wide, shallow bake pans are much better, as they expose larger bottoms to the fire and larger surfaces from which the sap can evaporate. Those huge iron pots hanging over the fire from metal tripods, such as the one seen in Currier & Ives prints of sugaring time in early New England, are very romantic in appearance, but terribly inefficient.

Usually I don't finish my syrup over the campfire, as there is too much risk of burning it. I reduce it to about twenty to one, at which point it is amber-colored, extremely sweet, but still watery thin. Then I move it to my kitchen stove for the final touches. It now takes only two gallons of this concentrated sap to make one gallon of syrup—and one gallon of water released as steam won't saturate the house, but will impart a fragrant and healthful humidity. As the boiling syrup approaches the proper consistency, it will boil over if not carefully watched. A few drops of cream or a little butter dropped into the pot will help to keep it under control. When the liquid reaches exactly 219 degrees on your candy thermometer you have syrup of perfect consistency.

If you want to try making maple sugar, keep the syrup cooking a bit longer. The boiling temperature will mount faster now, so keep your eye on that thermometer. When it reaches exactly 236 degrees, snatch it from the fire. Stir and beat until it begins to thicken, and you notice sugaring about the edges of the pan.

Then get it into molds as quickly as possible. Use cups, bowls, loaf pans, or muffin pans. When cooled, the sugar can be removed from the molds by slightly heating them in hot water.

Let's get back out in the woods. Which species of the maple should you tap? The answer to that one is easy: Tap any and all species available. Most maple syrup and sugar come from two species, the sugar maple, *Acer saccharum*, and the very closely related black maple, A. *nigrum*. Too few folks are aware that it is possible to use other maples for this purpose. While I was making my experiments, people were so skeptical of the worth of the sap from these unused species that I decided to attempt to settle the question. I kept separately the sap of each of the five species I was tapping, boiled exactly five gallons of each kind down to sugar, then tested the samples.

The sugar maple came in first in this maple marathon, but only by a nose. Strangely, it was an introduced tree, the Norway maple (A. *plataneides*) that came in a very close second. In third place was the common box elder (A. *negundo*), sometimes called the ash-leaved maple or the compound-leaf maple. Though I was raised a thousand miles from maple-sugaring country, I had known this tree all my life without suspecting that it was fairly bursting with sugar. In fourth place was the red maple or swamp maple (A. *rubrum*), and in last place was the silver maple (A. *saccarinum*), despite the fact that its botanical name means "sugary." Another panel of tasters, composed of friends, was unable to tell the difference betwen sugars from the various trees.

Many readers feel that they want to use professional equipment rather than improvise their gear as I do. Fortunately, I heard from a supplier of such equipment, Sugar Bush Supplies Co., Box 1107, Lansing, Michigan 48904, who say they have "Complete maple sugar-making and marketing equipment."

I also had a letter from a woman in Bellingham, Washington, who told me that she tapped the big-leaved maples (A. *macrophyllum*) of that area using sections of old plastic garden hose for spiles and plastic bleach bottles and mayonnaise jars for sap buckets.

Further, she wrote that she tapped a few striped maples (*A. pennsylvanicum*), a tree I thought too small to bother with. She admits the trees were small, but says they drip sap abundantly, and when she boiled this sap separately she found that it was very sweet, yielding more sugar per gallon than the larger maples. Her family also maintains that this little maple yields syrup of even better flavor than that of regular maples.

The sugar content of maple sap varies widely from tree to tree, as well as from species to species, so these results are not conclusive. But they do show that perfectly good syrup can be made from other maples than the sugar maple.

Other trees besides maples also produce sweet saps. I tap the butternuts and black walnuts at the same time I tap the maples, but never have boiled their sap separately, so can't say how rich they are in sugar. I tapped a sycamore or buttonwood (*Platanus occidentalis*), and was delighted with its copious flow. But alas, when I boiled five gallons of the sap, it yielded about two table-spoonfuls of syrup and tasted like a poor grade of blackstrap molasses. I concluded that the sycamore would furnish an excellent source of pure drinking water, but little else.

The birches all yield sweet sap, and I once spent several days collecting and boiling the sap of the black birch (*Betula lenta*). They start flowing about the time the maples stop, enabling one to extend the season. Birch syrup does not taste like maple, but is good enough in its own right. This sap is only about half as sweet as maple sap, and making the syrup is consequently twice as laborious.

There are reliable reports that excellent maple sugar can be made from the sugar tree, or southern sugar maple (*Acer barbatum*), which grows all over the south, and from the big-leaved maple (*A. macrophyllum*; see page 95) that grows in the Pacific Northwest. There are other reports, apparently not so reliable, that sugar-yielding sap can be tapped from the basswoods and hickories, but I have never been able to get a drop of sap from either genus.

Yet even without these doubtful species there are enough sugar-yielding trees about so that anyone who searches hard enough is likely to find one to tap.

14. Going Underground

NOT many people would consider a spade a piece of sporting equipment, but that's because very few have discovered that digging in uncultivated areas can be an excellent sport.

Though this pastime can be practiced any time the ground is not frozen, it is at its best for only a few days in early spring. When the frost first goes out of the ground, it leaves it soft, fluffy, and easy to dig—and at that time of year there is more to find. On the first warm day in March, I fill my pockets with plastic bags, shoulder a spade, and go out to see what's happening in the underground.

I don't have to travel to distant wilderness areas to practice this sport. In the center of a square formed by four fruit trees there is a pit where I compost my garbage. Last summer giant burdock (*Arctium*) grew luxuriantly around its edges. I find the remains of old, first-year leaves of this biennial, and shooting up from wintered-over roots are the first tightly rolled leaves of second-year foliage. Burdock is considered nothing but a pesky dooryard weed in this country, but is highly appreciated as a food plant in other areas of the world. I've eaten the young leaf stems, parboiled, battered, and fried, at the home of an excellent Italian cook, and found them delicious. They are slightly bitter, but it is a good bitter, and the Italians have learned to appreciate the subtleties of this flavor. In Japan, this same weed is cultivated as a root vegetable, called *gobo*, and it is considered a very healthful, strength-giving, and restorative food.

I have also eaten the roots of wild burdock in summer and fall, and found them very good food, but it is often brutal labor to dig deep for *gobo* in summer or fall, when the ground is hard. Now my spade slips into the softened earth as if it were a pile of sawdust, and I soon have dug up five large roots—more than a pound of *gobo*. I slice off the tender crowns, putting them in one plastic bag and the trimmed roots in another.

Nearby is a pile of wood chips I persuaded some tree trimmers to dump on my place, and around it dandelions grow to giant size. It is still too early for dandelion greens, as the tops have nothing on them but a few tough, reddish winter leaves, but it is roots I'm after, anyway. In this rich soil the roots are as large as good-sized carrots, and I soon have a dozen of them in another bag.

I don't entirely neglect the aboveground harvest, either. Winter cress or yellow rocket (*Barbarea verna*) finds the base of this chip pile a wonderful place to grow, too, and the greens on this member of the mustard family are in their prime. I love these vitamin-filled greens short-cooked and garnished with crumpled, crisp bacon, so I fill another bag.

There is a wild persimmon tree near the chip pile, one of several dozen that grow on my place. If unpicked, many of its fruits will cling to the tree all winter, growing sweeter and more luscious all the time, while losing every bit of the astringency that makes this fruit unpopular. I leave a few trees unpicked to serve as free cafeterias for persimmon eaters during the winter. Even in March, there are still hundreds of sweet little fruits at the top of the tree. I climb to the upper branches, recline against a large limb, and stuff myself with sugary fruit to give me energy to go on with my digging operations. While up there I fill a plastic bag with persimmons so the grounded members of the family can enjoy them. I realize that it is only the young and agile who can run up and down trees in search of wild fruits. Fortunately, I am only fifty-nine years old. In another twenty years I will have to begin easing off on this tree-climbing habit.

Down out of the tree, I walk across an old field where Queen Anne's lace bloomed in profusion last year. Here and there I see some feathery foliage just breaking through the soft ground. This weed is exactly the same species as our summer garden carrot, so whenever I see a last-year's sprouting, I shove down my spade. Some of these wild carrots are too small and stringy to bother about, so I take only the largest and fleshiest ones, filling another bag. Accidentally I turn up a red clover root while digging carrots, so I examine it. It's fleshy and looks edible—and I fill another bag.

Then I head for a patch of wild Jerusalem artichokes I noticed last fall while they were in bloom. The old six-foot-high stalks make them easy to locate now. The tubers are large and in perfect condition. I have a passion for artichoke pickles and want to make at least two quarts of them, so I fill two bags. The artichoke patch borders a marshy area on one side, and as I am digging on the edge of the marsh I turn up a string of ground-nuts, delectable little tubers the size of bantam eggs, several together on a string. I dig furiously in that area and soon have a bagful of these tasty tubers. Now I notice the whitish vines of the plant that bore them, twining around the artichoke stalks.

By this time I am loaded down and running out of plastic bags. I take a short cut toward home over a wooded hill. Near the top of the hill the wintergreen berries redden the ground, much fatter and sweeter than they were last fall. I like to nibble these teaberries for their pleasant wintergreen flavor as I walk through the woods. I also like to include them in a tossed salad to give an interesting taste and a Christmasy look. And a good jam can be made of these berries, if one knows exactly how to do it. No more plastic bags, so I fill my coat pockets and head home.

Dinner is a memorable meal with the first wild winter cress greens of the season. The groundnuts are washed, then sliced, peel and all, and fried slowly with a little vegetable oil in a covered skillet. They are excellent. After the dishes are out of the way, I take over the kitchen. The artichokes are peeled, then packed in quart jars. I pour a cup of cider vinegar in each jar, then fill with cold water, add one clove of garlic, one red pepper, and a teaspoon of dill seed. That's all. I just cover the jars and put them away to pickle.

I put two cups of washed wintergreen berries into the blender, add one cup of water, and run the machine on high speed a few minutes. Then I add the juice of one lemon and three cups of raw sugar. A package of commercial pectin is dissolved in three-fourths cup of water, then put on the fire and boiled hard for one minute. Next I add the pectin to the mixture in the blender, blend at slow speed for about one minute, then pour it into jars. I have to hurry at this stage, for the stuff threatens to jell before I can get it into those babyfood jars I use for jelly. This jelly retains the bright wintergreen flavor of the fresh fruit, for the berries are never cooked. It must be kept in the freezer for long storage, but an open jar will keep in the refrigerator for about three weeks.

Then I turned to my roots. I peel the burdock roots with an ordinary potato peeler and slice them thin across the grain. After boiling for fifteen minutes, they are tender. I salt and butter them and find they are not only edible, but very good. They taste a little like potato, but they still have a rather pleasant flavor that is all their own.

The little white carrots I scrape and boil. I'm surprised to find that each one has a tiny, woody core. Once this is removed, the rest of the boiled root is edible, with a familiar carroty taste, though they are not as sweet as garden carrots. Judging from their white color I would guess that they have very little, if any, vitamin A. My verdict is: not very good, but a vegetable that would be an asset to camp stew if no domestic carrots were available.

The dandelion roots are scraped and sliced, then boiled in salted water. These prove to be excellent. I think most people will appreciate this unique root vegetable at first taste. It has something of the flavor of dandelion greens, but the texture is a bit potato-like. Also, it is quite sweet, and I suspect that this root has a high sugar content.

I search through my wild-food library and discover that red clover roots are reputed to be edible. I scrape, slice, and boil them in salted water. Then I butter a serving of them generously and eagerly try this new dish. Hmmmm. Edible? Yes. Delicious? No. They taste good enough to interest a really hungry man, but I'm not that hungry. Red clover roots definitely could not be described as a delicacy. I decide I will continue to use red clover blossoms to make a smooth summer tea, but will leave the roots in the ground.

Soon I will be preparing the ground for my organic garden, but meanwhile there is great satisfaction in sharing the produce from God's garden. The price of partnership in this bountiful larder is a little knowledge and a willingness to listen to what nature has to say. I feel a little smug at being able to harvest organic vegetables before my friends have even begun to plant.

15. Spring, Spring, Spring!

NO one, but no one, enjoys seeing spring come more than I do. I love the other seasons, too, but I have special reasons to welcome spring. I try to organize my year so that my greatest writing tasks come in winter. Then, just as I bring a long written work to conclusion and feel a great sense of liberation, nature seems to stir to life and celebrate with me. Now is the time to stop writing about nature and get out into it. It is the season for research and exploration, a time of taking in, not putting out, and I revel in it.

My first spring vegetables are wild plants. I know where dandelion plants grow so luxuriantly that huge, tender crowns, which make four bites each when properly cleaned and boiled, can be cut from the tops of roots. These dandelion roots are as large as good-sized carrots. When peeled, then sliced and boiled or sautéed, they serve up as a fine root vegetable, much superior to parsnips to my taste.

Along small streams I gather the thick, kidney-shaped leaves of the marsh marigold, boil them through two waters to remove part of the pungency, then eat them with gobs of butter. Tender and tasty poke sprouts appear on my table long before the first asparagus is ready. Up on the little mountain back of my house the wintergreen berries are brighter, fatter, and juicier in early spring than they were last fall. A few of them in a watercress salad make a dish appetizingly beautiful, while adding a taste of wintergreen I love.

Contrary to accusations that have often been made, I do not see nature *only* as a vast storehouse of gourmet food. Early spring gladdens my soul at the same time that it tickles my appetite. I know a secret place where lilac-colored hepaticas bloom before any other wild flower can be found. In a nearby abandoned field, grape hyacinths have become naturalized and now cover acres of south slope with a carpet of beauty. Between my house and mailbox there is a bank that is covered with windflowers (anemones) every spring. I have knelt in wonder before the beautiful, shell-like spathe of the skunk cabbage, and watched the first bee of the season wade knee-deep in the bright-yellow pollen that covered the spadix, accumulating such a load of this gold of spring that he had difficulty flying away with it.

Then there is coltsfoot. I find it hard to explain my inordinate love for this common plant of such ordinary appearance. Partly it is because coltsfoot is often the first plant to shout out that spring is coming. The little flower stalks, resembling tiny asparagus shoots, sometimes appear as early as February. When the flower opens, coltsfoot stops pretending to be miniature asparagus and starts to mimic the dandelion, to which it is actually related. The flower is somewhat similar to the dandelion in color, form and size, and even turns into the same kind of fuzzball when it seeds. It is only after the flowers are all gone that the leaves tardily appear, springing from separate buds on the perennial root. These leaves are large, two to six inches across, and the plant gets its name because the outline of the leaf is thought to resemble the track of a young horse.

Another reason I am so fond of coltsfoot may be that I know it, as I know many other wild plants, by taste as well as by sight. Its botanical name, *Tussilage*, means cough dispeller, for ever

Coltsfoot.

since ancient Greek and Roman days the leaves have been considered the most eminent of herbal remedies for treating a cough.

To make coltsfoot cough drops, cover an ounce of fresh coltsfoot leaves with one pint of water and boil down until only a cupful of the liquid is left. Strain and discard the spent leaves.

To the cupful of liquid add two cups of raw or brown sugar, then boil until a drop of the syrup forms a hard ball when dropped into cold water. Pour onto a buttered cookie sheet and score into coughdrop sizes before it hardens. I often wonder if the popularity of coltsfoot as a cough remedy is not due as much to its flavor as to its efficacy, for it is the most palatable of all cough medicines. Ofttimes I eat a coltsfoot coughdrop purely for pleasure, even when I have no cough.

To keep coltsfoot leaves all year, spread them on papers in a warm attic, dry them until they crumble, then store in tight jars to preserve the flavor. To make coltsfoot tea, cover a table-spoonful of the leaves with a cup of boiling water and steep for about three minutes, then sweeten with honey to taste. It is not only good for a cough—it is good.

Pliny, the great first-century naturalist of Rome, gives directions for smoking coltsfoot that make it sound like a religious rite. He directed that the smoker drop dried coltsfoot leaves onto burning cypress charcoal, then inhale the smoke through a hollow reed, taking a sip of wine between puffs. This was recommended for every chest ailment from "humours and distillations on the lungs" to wheezes and stitches in the side. My lungs felt fine when I first came across this information, but the directions sounded so delightfully orgiastic that I couldn't resist trying them. I charred a bit of cypress knee (a root knob showing above swamp water), took a glass of rare old dandelion wine and some dried coltsfoot leaves, and repaired to a sylvan dell surrounded by the wild flowers of early spring. On an altar-shaped rock I built a tiny fire of cypress charcoal, dropped on the dried leaves, and duly puffed and sipped the wine. I felt that such a ceremony should inspire something creative, maybe an original pastoral dance or symphony. But my interests lie in other directions. When I emerged from the fumes of coltsfoot and dandelion, I found a verse written in my notebook!

16. Stalking the Wild Et Cetera

I AM writing this article near the end of May, a perfect
spring day—no day to be chained to a typewriter, but a
deadline approaches. Procrastinating right up to the last minute,
I told my wife that I needed to take a walk before beginning the
day's writing. At this time of year the growth of wild plants is so
swift that I can see a great difference in the heights of individual
plants from only a few days before. Thistles that had shown
nothing but a rosette of leaves flat on the ground last week now
have flower stalks as much as eighteen inches high.

Recently I became very much interested in this pesky weed. I
read an account by Truman C. Everts of how he had been lost in
the wilderness of the Yellowstone region of Wyoming in 1870.
He went thirty-seven days with no food but thistle roots, yet he
survived and was able to travel to the vicinity of a settlement
before being found.

Dr. George Washington Carver, in *Nature's Garden for Vic-
tory and Peace*, says that thistle leaves are a good cooked vegetable if the spines are trimmed off with a pair of scissors. A

number of other writers, both in Europe and in America, have recommended the elongating young stems, peeled and boiled.

Once I tried the roots in very early spring, when the first little thistle leaves betrayed their hiding places. Among the several species that were sprouting then, I found that all had edible roots, but those of the common thistle, *Cirsium vulgare*, were best, if only because they were larger and consequently less tedious to prepare. Some of these roots were ten to twelve inches long, spindle-shaped—that is, larger in the middle and tapering toward either end—and as much as ¾-inch in diameter. Paring off the outside, then cutting the root into ¼-inch disks, crosswise, I boiled them for twenty minutes. Seasoned with salt and butter, they made an excellent dish. Several guests tried them, and all pronounced them very good.

This morning after my find I went back to the house for a stout pair of plastic gloves, a knife, a pair of scissors, and a supply of plastic bags. I'm afraid that trimming stickers off thistle leaves will never become popular. Those sharp spines penetrated even plastic gloves enough so that I could feel them, and trimming the leaves was a tedious task with little left to show for the effort. The rapid-growing flower stalk was another matter. This peeled very easily and left me with a tender heart about an inch in diameter and a foot long. It had a hole up the center, but this hollow wasn't very large. I filled a bag with these peeled stalks.

Returning home meant going to work, so I wandered on to a little clearing that has in it a pile of black, rotted sawdust, where a sawmill stood some fifty years ago. The area has grown up in poke (*Phytolacca americana*) and in that rich soil it was two feet high already, with stalks an inch and a half in diameter. I recalled that I had seen country people in southern Indiana eat these stalks with great gusto when they were peeled and fried. When I told someone of this a few days ago, he asked me if these same peeled stalks wouldn't make a good boiled vegetable. I had to confess that the only boiled poke stalks I had ever eaten were

Field Sow Thistle.

the shorter ones of the early sprouts—which I cook like asparagus—and that these were excellent. I simply didn't know
whether these big, fat stalks would be good boiled, but since I
was stalking things this morning I decided to find out. Another
bag was soon filled with peeled poke stalks, and I took along
some of the leaves from the very tops of the stalks.

Around the edges of this rich clearing were growing many tall
plants of sow thistle (*Sonchus oleraceus*) which isn't a thistle at
all, and doesn't have anything to do with a sow. These had put
on more growth in a week than any other plant observed, for the
week before they had displayed nothing but a rosette of dande-
lion-like leaves, and now the developing flower stalk stood waist-
high. Actually, this plant is a close, though overgrown, relative
of the dandelion, and, for that matter, of garden lettuce. I had
eaten the boiled greens before, in Maine, where this plant is
often found growing in the debris at high-tide level. Up there it is
often called "beach lettuce." That specific name, *oleraceus*,
could be roughly translated to mean "good enough to be a garden vegetable," so apparently this plant has been eaten by others
before.

I began to peel the tender stalks, and soon found that the
walls of the larger ones were too thin to furnish much food.
After they were peeled, one had little left besides a long slender
hole. But the younger ones, stout but only a foot or so high, still
had almost solid centers. These peeled easily, so I filled another
plastic bag. The leaves at the top of the still lengthening flower
stalk were so tender that they could easily be pinched off their
stems. These leaves somewhat resemble thistle leaves without the
prickly spines, and this probably is the origin of that common
name, but this plant is no thistle. Later it will produce flowers
that closely resemble dandelions in size, shape, and color, but
they will be on a long flower stalk up to three or four feet from
the ground. Even the leaves more closely resemble giant dandelion leaves than thistle leaves to my eyes. I filled another bag
with the tender leaves.

Returning home with my loot, I persuaded my wife that I

should cook these delicacies for lunch before starting to write. Sometimes I think I would make an excellent con man, a much more lucrative profession than the one I am in. The greens went into three pots and the stalks into three more, for I wanted to taste each separately. All the greens were cooked about fifteen minutes, then drained, salted, and buttered. The thistle leaves were the best of the cooked greens, almost good enough to make all that trimming worthwhile. The poke was good, as always, but since this time I had cooked only the very tenderest, youngest, topmost leaves from the plant, they were even better than usual. The sow thistle was a bit bitter, but it was a good bitter, like dandelion greens, with a hint of artichoke flavor, and another indefinable flavor that is very good and all its own. After tasting all three, I blended them together into a superior vegetable dish.

To prepare the thistle stalks, I peeled and washed them and then sliced them crosswise—because of the hollow center they became little O's. These were boiled twenty minutes and seasoned with salt, butter, and a dash of mixed herbs. They were even better than the thistle roots, with much the same delicate artichoke flavor. This is a mild, tender vegetable, and I don't see how anyone could dislike it. It is far better than many vegetables that we laboriously grow and regularly bring to our tables. The thistle is a pest in pasturelands, and maybe eating it is the right way to control it.

A thin outside rind from the poke stalks was peeled, then they were sliced diagonally and boiled for ten minutes and seasoned the same way. Here is a vegetable that beats asparagus. It is delicate, mild, and delicious, a dish that could grace any table in the land.

Those peeled sow thistle stalks were cooked in the same way, and they were great. I like the peeled stalks much better than I do sow thistle greens. The greens may be "soul food," but the peeled stalks, boiled only a few minutes, then buttered, are a gourmet food.

After I finish this writing, I am going over to another old

abandoned sawmill I know and gather all the fat stalks of poke I can find. I'll peel them and cut them into four-inch lengths, blanch these pieces for three minutes in boiling water, then quickly cool them in cold water, drain, package, and freeze them. Then when you visit me I won't have to tell you how good poke stalks are, I can show you. While I'm about it, I'll freeze a few packages of thistle stems and sow thistle stems, too. I don't know of better vegetables with which to fill up my freezer. All to be had for the taking from God's own supply; He happens to be my favorite gardener.

I'll need to save a little room in the freezer. In about two weeks the flower stalks of burdock will be just right for the harvest. Then I'll have more feasts and fill more freezer containers. These stalks must be gathered when they first spring up and while they are still tender. Peel off all the shreddy rind and slice them rather thin, crosswise. Then boil for at least forty-five minutes. They are starchy and potato-like, but they don't cook apart like potatoes, and they have a unique and delicious flavor. To freeze them, blanch for fifteen minutes, then cool, package, and hurry into the quick-freeze section of your freezer.

Truly, "stalking" is a grand outdoor sport, and leads one into some rare taste thrills.

Poke or Indian poke—which one can we eat? Since I first wrote about poke, several people have reminded me that there are two plants called "poke" in this country, and the unwary might confuse the edible pokeweed, poke-salad or inkberry, with the poisonous Indian poke or white hellebore, *Veratrum viride*. While I feel a bit like the man who was asked to write a treatise on how to tell a crow from a crocus, I'll try to clear up this not-so-difficult question.

The only way these two vastly different plants even remotely resemble one another is in those unfortunate common names. No one who knows either plant—however slightly—could ever mistake one for the other. They look nothing alike, grow in different habitats, and appear at different seasons. Pokeweed or inkberry first produces asparagus-like fat sprouts that spring from the crown of a massive perennial root. These sprouts are topped by pointed leaves, and they grow rapidly into a very coarse, purple-stemmed herb up to eight or ten feet tall, producing long clusters of purple-black berries opposite the leaves. It grows in rich, open, well-drained soil of farmyards, recent clearings, and around cultivated fields.

White hellebore (let's stop calling it Indian poke and clear up this confusion) grows in wet meadows, marshes, low woods and along streams, in very wet habitats. It is the first thing up in the spring, and I doubt that it was ever eaten because it was mistaken for pokeweed. The trouble is that its first little columnar stems with their tightly rolled leaves are a beautiful succulent green and look eminently edible to the uninitiated food gatherer out looking for potherbs in the very early spring. These leaves quickly unroll and grow to the size of elephant's ears. They are longitudinally fluted or corrugated, arranged spirally on an elongating stem that finally produces a greenish inflorescence—all before the first pokeweed shoots get out of the ground.

I know you won't try to eat white hellebore, but if any of your not-so-well-informed friends are rash enough to try it, cardiac and respiratory stimulants should be given. This plant produces a drug that is a valuable reducer of blood pressure, but a plateful of cooked white hellebore could reduce your blood pressure to zero. Fortunately, the poison is usually spontaneously vomited, so it is difficult to hold down a fatal dose, but anyone who eats white hellebore is in for a very uncomfortable time, at the least.

Being afraid to eat pokeweed, or inkberry, because a very dissimilar plant, sometimes called Indian poke, is poisonous would be like refusing to eat apples because a poisonous South American plant is called Apple of Peru. Anyone whose eyes are so poorly trained as to be unable to distinguish between such vastly different plants should not be allowed to gather vegetables from the vegetable garden, or even to go shopping for them, let alone gather food from the wild.

17. Where the Sweetest Berries Grow

DON'T try to tell me that wild berries are too tedious to pick to be worth the gathering. Although in my own garden I raise strawberries, blueberries, red raspberries, and gooseberries, having this domestic fruit available doesn't interfere with my wild-berry picking.

Indeed, I'm sometimes tempted to abandon all efforts to raise berries—since the wild plants produce better fruit that comes to me much easier with far less work than what I grow. To raise domestic berries successfully one must dig, transplant, fertilize, weed, cultivate, and prune—and, finally, pick. Wild berries are sometimes hard to find and tedious to gather, but when I reflect that I have not put in one minute's work before coming to harvest them, I am more willing to put some extra time and effort into the actual picking.

Seldom do I think of wild and domestic fruits as being in competition with one another. I love to gorge myself on the huge strawberries from my garden, but a dish of the ultra-sweet and highly fragrant tiny wild strawberries is a totally different experience. And those almost plum-sized blueberries from my hybrid bushes make a very good dessert fruit, but let's be honest, most of the extra size is made up of pure water .When used in baking, such oversized berries burst, discoloring muffins and causing them to stick to the pan. The smaller wild blueberries are sweeter, drier, and more concentrated, and make far better blueberry muffins.

Then, too, I value the domestic red raspberries as fresh fruit, for shortcake and as jam timber, yet I don't consider them a substitute for the wild blackcaps or black raspberries that grow outside my garden and make the most delightful-tasting jam ever eaten with a hot biscuit. I let the large Poorman gooseberries in my garden get purply-ripe before using them as fresh fruit or making some truly outstanding gooseberry pie, but the smaller wild gooseberries—both the prickly and the smooth kinds—are picked while still underripe, then used to make a tangy, tart sauce to eat with meat—a sauce that is so good it almost makes cranberry sauce seem too plebeian to deserve respect.

Actually I begin picking berries about the time the last spring snow melts away. Wintergreen berry, or teaberry, flourishes in the acid soil of mixed forests that cover the hills in this part of Pennsylvania. These cling all winter to the tiny evergreen plants that produce them and are fatter, juicier, and tastier by early spring than they were back in the fall. I love their vague sweetness and sprightly wintergreen flavor. Some I eat fresh, some I glacé in lemon-flavored syrup, but mostly I use them in salads.

The first tender spring growth of wild watercress liberally sprinkled with bright-red wintergreen berries and seasoned with an oil and vinegar dressing into which a bit of wild garlic has been crushed is quite beautiful and as good as it looks. If you dislike such a creation, you should trade your taste buds in on some new ones!

Teaberries can usually be picked until about the time that wild strawberries appear. Surely I don't have to tell anyone what to do with wild strawberries. My family—with my help, of course—can eat all I pick. However, I do fight them off from a few quarts so I can make some wild strawberry jam, using a method where the berries are never cooked. Such jam must be kept in the freezer to preserve it, but it is a joy to open a jar in midwinter and be greeted with all the flavor and fragrance of the fresh fruit. I also enjoy the fresh frozen fruit, too, if I manage to save enough from my friends and family to freeze.

By the time the last strawberry has been picked, the first wild raspberries appear. I love to eat this fruit fresh from the bush, but consider it too seedy to be an ideal table berry. I put the fruit through the vegetable juicer a quart at a time, then make a seedless jam of the thick, semi-solid juice. Again, this is prepared by a no-cook method that preserves all the flavor of the fresh berry.

Before the black raspberries are gone, nature has begun a regular festival of berries which will last the summer. One of my favorites is the relative of the raspberry, the wineberry. Botanically, this recent immigrant from Asia has the almost unpronounceable name *Rubus phoenicolasius*. Apparently introduced in eastern Pennsylvania in the late nineteenth century, it promptly went wild and made itself thoroughly at home. Still spreading, the wineberry is becoming common over a fairly wide area. I have picked this berry in Pennsylvania, New Jersey, Delaware, Maryland, and Virginia. Look for it in your section. You may be missing a good thing.

The wineberry is produced on large, bristly canes up to ten feet long. Like those of the black raspberry, these canes are inclined to bend over and take root at the tip, producing almost impenetrable briar patches. The bloom is insignificant, and the berry is borne inside the husklike calyx until it is full size. Then the calyx opens and the berry ripens. Orange-red in color, it resembles a raspberry and has a clammy, sticky feel. A dish of sweetened wineberries, covered with cream, is a rare treat. They make pretty good jam, but I like the fresh fruit so well that I freeze all the surplus that I can gather to enjoy fresh wineberries all winter.

Together, blackberries and dewberries probably comprise our most valuable wild-food crop, thousands of tons of wild berries being picked and sold in markets every year. The difference between them is that dewberries are borne on trailing repine vines and blackberries on stiff canes. No two taxonomists are able to agree on the number of species of either that is found in this bountiful land of ours.

I have picked blackberries literally from coast to coast and border to border, gathering them in Texas and Maine, in California and Washington, and even in the hills of the island of Maui in Hawaii. A summer without picking wild blackberries would seem like a year wasted. I use them fresh, make pies and jam, and especially like blackberry flummery—another Scandinavian-type fruit soup thickened with cornstarch, and not too sweet. It's eaten either before meals as a soup, or after meals as a dessert.

Long before the last blackberries are gone, the blueberries and huckleberries are begging to be picked, and they, too, are especially prolific here in central Pennsylvania. In this section all such fruits are called "huckleberries"—as many as five species often being mixed in the same pail. Since they are all equally delicious, no one cares. Those who like to be more precise reserve the name "blueberry" for blue or bluish-black members of the genus *Vaccinium*, and use the term huckleberry for berries of the genus *Gaylussacia*. If you really want to know which genus the berry you have belongs to, open it and look at the seeds. Blueberries or *Vaccinium* species have many soft seeds, while huckleberries, or *Gaylussacia* species, have exactly ten hard, seedlike nutlets inside.

Whether they are blueberries or huckleberries, everyone knows they make the finest pies ever eaten by man. Wonderful fresh, served with either plain or whipped cream, they are also easily frozen, so there is little excuse for not having enough in the freezer to last until next season. All I do is pick them over and put them, dry, into jars and set them in the freezer. Being

Squaw Huckleberry.

dry, they don't even stick together as they freeze, and I can open a jar and simply pour out a cupful of frozen berries whenever I get a hankering for some blueberry muffins.

Don't overlook the squaw huckleberry or deerberry. Although more closely related to the blueberries than to the huckleberries (its botanical name is *Vaccinium staminium*) the fruit is quite different from either of them. The berries are more than twice as large as the average wild blueberry, somewhat pear-shaped and greenish-yellow in color when ripe. On the rocky ridge behind our house, these sometimes bear so profusely that the weight of the fruit pulls the thin bushes to the ground. As raw, fresh fruit the squaw huckleberry is almost inedible, being slightly bitter. But it makes a uniquely flavored jam that is a double threat, being good on toast, biscuits, or muffins for breakfast and also good as a sauce for meat, fish, or fowl. If you have plenty of squaw huckleberries and don't think they are worth picking, call me.

Elderberry.

And, of course, there is the ubiquitous elderberry, nodding those great umbels of blue-black berries, inviting you to take them as a gift from Mother Nature. You don't have to make wine of them, for elderberries make a fine jelly, and properly treated are the equal of huckleberries as pie material. Most of my neighbors make pies of the fresh fruit, adding vinegar to the mix, for elderberries need extra acid. But the finest elderberry pies are made of the half-dried fruit. I spread elderberries on an old screen door, put them out in the sun, and when they are just dry enough to start wrinkling I put them in jars and freeze them like blueberries. Even these need vinegar or lemon juice added to the pie mix, but with this addition elderberry pies become habit-forming. Once you have learned to like them, you will find yourself thinking of elderberry pie about once a week, so freeze plenty of berries.

Even my close neighbors, who are country people, often ask me how I manage to find so many wild berries. I don't just wait until the proper season and then go out looking for ripe berries. By that time I already know where they are. The secret is in thinking a bit wild all year. On every country walk I note where all the berry plants grow. On every drive my eye takes in the berrying possibilities and other wild-food prospects as I pass by. My wife long ago decided that my interest in wayside plants was a major hazard when I was behind the wheel, so she took over the driving, leaving me free to give my full attention to the wild edibles that grow along every country road. When berries bloom, they are most conspicuous, and it is then that I make mental notes to return to the best patches when the berries are ripe. Once a good berry patch is located, it will often continue to bear for many years. Gradually, a map of all the finest berry-picking territory in this area has developed in my mind.

Even if picking wild berries were more work than raising your own, which it is not, I would still go for these wildings. One sees and experiences so much more than merely the berries one picks. Pheasants skyrocket out of cover before you, a deer walks by, or a mother grouse leads her young out to parade for your approval, sometimes with the belligerent little father along for protection. He spreads his tail and drags his wingtips, looking for all the world like a turkey gobbler. One notes patches of Jerusalem artichokes and resolves to be back in October for another harvest. And nature always makes some unexpected gifts—an Indian cucumber, a tender cat-brier tip, or some other unexpected nibble.

Picking wild berries is an ideal way to establish an intimate and meaningful relationship with nature. All the pleasures you enjoyed on the balmy summer days when you gathered them will come flooding back into mind when you eat your frozen trophies in midwinter. Those berries from my freezer not only bear the special flavor of wild fruit, they bear the flavor of summer. They give nourishment to my body, taste thrills to my palate, and food for my soul. Thank God for wild berries.

18. The Dill Crock

EVERY wild-food gatherer needs a dill crock. Every gardener needs a dill crock. Everybody needs one.

And just what is a dill crock? It is a way to enjoy some of the finest food you ever tasted. It is an "in" thing with as much status value as a free-form swimming pool—but costs practically nothing. It's the way to practice one-upmanship on a budget. It is a grand luxury that soon becomes a necessity. A dill crock is so easily made and maintained that there is no excuse for not having one. One? After getting started on this hobby, I'll bet you make two, or three, or maybe a half-dozen.

Naturally I got started on this tasty sport with wild foods. A nearby patch of wild Jerusalem artichokes had yielded a bumper crop, and I wanted some artichoke pickles. I didn't even use a crock; I used a gallon-size glass jar. (I get all the jars I want from a nearby school cafeteria, which purchases salad dressing in them.)

It was late fall, and my dill bed had long since gone to seed— so long ago, in fact, that a new volunteer crop of dill had sprung up. It wasn't flowering, but it did have the right aroma and flavor, so I decided to use it, anyway, adding a few dill seeds to make sure.

Jerusalem Artichoke.

Packing a layer of dill at the bottom of the jar, I added several cloves of garlic, a few red tabasco peppers, then some peeled tubers of the Jerusalem artichokes plus another layer of dill. There was room left, and I looked around for other things to add. The winter onions had great bunches of top sets, so I peeled a few and made a layer of them. Then I dug up some of the bottom bulbs, which are shaped like huge cloves of garlic, to make another layer. I then made a layer of cauliflower picked apart into small florets and added some sweet red pepper cut into strips, along with a handful or two of green nasturtium seed pods.

This was all covered with brine made of one measure of salt to a half measure of vinegar and ten measures of water. I topped the whole thing with another layer of the young dill, set a small saucer on top weighted with a rock, to keep everything below the brine, and took it down in the cool cellar.

After two weeks I became impatient and broke into the hoard. The Jerusalem artichoke tubers were crisp and delicious. The winter onions, both top and bottom bulbs, were the best pickled onions I ever have tasted. The cauliflower florets all disappeared the first time I let my grandchildren taste them, while the nasturtium pods made better capers than capers. We had caper sauce, caper stuffing, and just plain capers.

The next year I determined to get started early and keep a huge dill crock going all season. Any size crock can be used, from one-gallon up. I use a ten-gallon crock and wish it were bigger. Never try to use a set recipe for the ingredients of a dill crock—let each one be a separate and original creation. I plant plenty of dill, and when it flowers I stuff the flower heads into plastic bags and put them in my freezer, where they will be good as fresh dill for up to a year.

And what is good in a dill crock? Nearly any kind of fresh, crisp vegetable. Green beans are perfect, and wax beans are also very good. These are the only two things I cook before dilling. Even these should be cooked only about three minutes, just enough to take the fuzziness off. One can't have *too* many dilled green beans. I believe I could use a whole crock of nothing else and still run out of green beans before the next season produced more.

Small green tomatoes are also great in this cure. I planted some cherry tomatoes last year and still had a lot of green ones when frost threatened. I cheated Jack Frost by gathering them and putting them down in the dill crock. Not only did they get used, they didn't even last until Thanksgiving. And nothing so nice ever happened to a head of cauliflower. Just break it up into small florets and drop it into the dilled brine. In a week or two you have the finest dilled cauliflower pickle ever tasted.

If you have winter onions (and if you don't, why don't you?) clean some of the top sets or bottom cloves and drop them in. Cleaning top sets is a tedious job, but worth it. Not only do they add to the flavor of all the rest of the ingredients of the crock, but the little onions themselves are a gourmet's delight. If you have no garden, you can still sometimes buy winter onions on the market. If you can't find them, just take ordinary small onions and slice them crosswise into from two to four pieces. Sure, they will come apart, but you'll have some mighty good pickled onion rings. I have even cut off the white part of scallions and put them in with some success. One fall the dill crock was flavored with white sections of leeks, and it was wonderful.

Some of my friends have experimented with adding things to the dill crock that I would never have thought of using. A woman I know peeled some zucchini squash and cut them crosswise into inch-thick chunks and dilled them. She recently brought me a sample, and they were so good that I "ate myself full," as my Pennsylvania Dutch neighbors would say. Another friend, this time a man, used up the last of his dilled vegetables and looked about for something with which to refill his crock. It was late summer, and watermelons were being sold at give-away prices. He bought several, peeled off just the outer green skin, then sliced them crosswise into inch-thick slices. Each of these slices was quartered and these quarters were dropped into fresh brine. The sugar in the melons apparently speeded the process, for in just four days he had some wonderful dilled food. Of course, he didn't add any garlic, onion, or any other flavoring besides dill. Dilled watermelon slices are real gourmet food.

There are refinements and tricks that can be used in maturing a perfect dill crock. A few grape leaves from either wild or domesticated vines improve the flavor and furnish exactly the right ferment to make it cure properly. A sprig of cherry leaves —from either wild or orchard trees—adds an epicurean flavor. While gathering cherry leaves to go into a crock, I wondered how dilled cherries would taste. Our Queen Annes were just developing a becoming blush, so I gathered a small pailful and dumped them in with the other ingredients, onions, garlic, peppers, and all. They took several weeks to cure properly, but were

Purslane.

worth the wait. Don't think of dilled cherries as cherries. Use and serve them like olives and call them "cherry olives." They are as elegant as champagne and caviar.

Cheered by this success, a few weeks later I tried peaches.

I gathered a pailful of ripe, but still firm, peaches, peeled and halved them, and packed them in dill and brine. They were excellent and seemed to be just right with the other dilled vegetables. And be sure to include some of those nasturtium seed pods mentioned before. You can use either the green, tender pods or the unopened flower buds. For that matter, the leaves have the same flavor. The buds and pods are even better than capers, and they also impart a subtle pungency to the other ingredients of the dill crock. I long ago stopped thinking of nasturtium buds as substitutes for capers. Now, if I am forced to use real capers because I have used up the nasturtium pods and buds, I think of the capers as substitutes for the nasturtium products.

Don't overlook the weeds as you build a dill crock. Young, tender sprouts of pokeberry plant with the outside peel removed make a wonderful layer in the dill crock. Even better is a layer of tender purslane stems (*Portulaca oleracea*). Remove the leaves from the succulent purple stems and just lay the stems in the crock. They become crisp and delicious, and we find them favorites as hors d'oeuvres and for light afternoon snacks for the young when you don't want them spoiling their appetites for dinner.

My grandchildren often forage their between-meal snacks. One of their favorites from late May until mid-July is the fat, tender new sprouts of the greenbrier, or catbrier (*Smilax rotundifolia*). They break these off only as low as they are tender and crisp and eat them, leaves, tendrils, and all. For some unfathomable reason they call this snack "bread-and-butter." When I asked why, they said they called it this because they ate it between meals, but I can't remember ever seeing my grandchildren eat plain bread and butter between meals.

When they discovered my dill crock, they wanted to know if I could dill their favorite wild tidbit. One can only try, so I sent them out to gather a supply. An hour later they were back with three plastic bags stuffed with the tender sprouts. I put half of them in raw, and boiled the other half for about ten minutes, and made another layer of them. They were somewhat different from one another, but both kinds made excellent dill pickles.

How do you use all these great masses of dilled vegetables? If you think they will become a problem, I suggest you borrow my grandchildren for a few days. They can make a crock of dilled vegetables disappear so fast you would think they were stage magicians. Don't think of the crock as a mighty jar of pickled condiments. Serve great bowls of dilled vegetables for lunch or dinner. Bring out a bowlful when serving drinks to guests, even if the drinks are no more than lemonade or cups of tea. Have a bowlful on a lunch or dinner buffet. Serve them at parties. Do you feel too lazy to make a dish for that covered-dish supper?

Just take a huge bowlful of dilled vegetables and bask in the praise you will receive.

Those on reducing diets, or diabetics on strict diets, will especially appreciate the hostess who serves dilled vegetables as refreshments. They are low in calories and are on the diabetic's "free" list.

How about putting whole large cucumbers and large green tomatoes in the dill crock? I make my dill pickles and dilled green tomatoes separately, as it takes these large vegetables a long time to cure properly. For the mixed dill crock I use only tiny cherry tomatoes and chunked or sliced cucumbers. Usually, I peel large cucumbers, cut them in thin sticks, and slice off the seed side. These will be delicious in less than a week.

I seldom have trouble with a dill crock but, judging from the letters I receive, some of my readers do have minor troubles. Always weight the vegetables down, with a plate or a rock, so they will stay below the top of the brine. The curing is a kind of fermentation, so don't think they are spoiled because you see bubbles. A thin scum on top of the brine means nothing. This is caused by some of the products of fermentation. Skim it off and go ahead and eat the vegetables. If a thicker scum persists on reappearing every time you skim it off, then remove the vegetables, rinse them in cold water, pack them in big jars with new brine and keep in the refrigerator until used. With these precautions you should never lose a jar of vegetables.

Want to do something special with dilled vegetables? How about some dilly rollups? Cut the crusts from slices of bread, spread the soft inside of each slice with mayonnaise, put a dilled green bean, a thin slice of dilled cucumber, or almost anything else you can fish out of the crock on the bread and roll gently, securing with a toothpick. Then cut each roll into three pieces, brush with melted butter, and quickly brown under the broiler. This makes one of the most elegant hot hors d'oeuvres ever invented.

19. The Teas of Revolution

AMERICAN history is steeped in tea. Colonial Americans were lusty drinkers of this bracing brew. We might still be a nation of great tea drinkers if the Revolution had not intervened. Tea played such a large role in our fight for independence that this struggle has been called The Tea War.

The British tried to assert their right to tax the colonies by placing a levy on tea—and the Americans refused to pay it. At first the struggle took the form of nonviolent resistance. The colonists simply refused to drink the taxed tea and started searching their own native flora for palatable substitutes. And they found them, in large numbers and wide variety. British attempts to collect the tea tax forcibly led to armed clashes, and these led directly into battles that finally resulted in the founding of a great new nation with drastically altered beverage habits.

Sassafras tea became a favorite beverage during the Great Tea War. It is made from the roots of a small native tree, *Sassafras albidum*, that grows abundantly from Maine to Florida and west to the Great Plains. The tree is easily recognized by

Sassafras.

having three kinds of leaves—unlobed, mitten-shaped, and double-thumb mitten-shaped—all growing at the same time. If there is any doubt about recognition, dig a root and smell it. The root beer aroma is unmistakable.

Some purists make sassafras tea from only the bark of the roots, but I use the whole root, merely washing and chopping it into pieces that will fit into a kettle. A pound of roots will easily make a gallon of tea, and the same roots can be used many times before they lose their strength. Just boil until the tea has a reddish-amber color, a heady aroma, and a pleasant taste. Some like it with sugar or honey, some with milk, some with both, and some with neither. Personally, I take it any way I can get it.

While searching for tea substitutes, some colonists came on the *Solidago odora*, or sweet goldenrod. It resembles other goldenrods, but when one of the slender, untoothed leaves is crushed, it emits the sweet odor of anise. Tea made from the dried leaves proved so good that most people preferred it to Oriental tea. These early Americans were an audacious lot, so after the Revolution they gathered a quantity of this tea and shipped it to China. When the tea connoisseurs of the Celestial Empire tasted this new beverage, they offered to trade almost any amount of their own tea for a single pound of these precious leaves. It is still appreciated in many sections where it grows. A neighbor here in central Pennsylvania gathers this tea every year and has no trouble disposing of it at several dollars per pound.

The patriots of New Jersey turned to a plant that is still known as New Jersey Tea (*Ceanothus americanus*), although it grows in gravelly soils throughout the eastern half of our nation. Each spring the woody, perennial red roots send up new leafy stems about three feet high, topped in June and July by attractive clusters of white flowers. The leaves are somewhat heart-shaped and grayish-green in color. The seed pods are triangular in shape when viewed from above. Then it is time to gather the leaves and dry them indoors. The tea resembles Oriental tea in flavor, is made the same way, and even imparts the same clean, rough feeling to the tongue. It contains no harmful drugs or stimulants, so you can drink all you want, and even serve it to children.

Teas made from members of the mint family, such as peppermint, spearmint, sage, catnip, and horehound, had long been popular in England. These plants were thoroughly naturalized in this country, growing wild in most of the colonies, and since the English didn't try to tax them, rebel Americans could drink them without being unpatriotic. Peppermint and spearmint teas have long been known as home remedies for upset stomach, but they could make palatable beverages, aiding digestion, sweetening the breath, and blending tastefully with many kinds of food.

Horehound tea is reputed to relieve coughs and allay fevers, but there is nothing to prevent your drinking this tea when you are healthy. Most of us acquired a taste for its bitter-aromatic flavor in early childhood by sucking on horehound drops.

The mythical Fountain of Youth must have been filled with sage tea, for old herbalists claimed that it would prevent ageing, restore youth, and even make gray hair resume its original color. I like its spicy, minty flavor when made with fresh, green sage leaves, but I'm still not as young as I used to be.

Catnip tea used to be given to babies as a home remedy for colic, and many of them grew up with a taste for its musky, aromatic flavor. It is reported to dispel nervousness and promote sleep, and would certainly be a safer remedy than the drug tranquilizers so widely misused today. Fresh catnip is rich in vitamin C, and it must have prevented many cases of scurvy among the American colonists.

Early tea hunters found two excellent beverages among the native American members of the mint family. Either the fresh or the dried leaves of *Monarda didyma*, commonly called Oswego tea or bee balm, make a fragrant brew that must have perfumed many Colonial kitchens. The other was American pennyroyal, *Hedeoma pulegiodes*. This is a thin, branching plant which, unlike most members of the mint family, prefers to grow on dry, gravelly hills in poor soil. It loves sterile acid ground and is usually abundant about old sawmills. The dried leaves make a highly flavored and very fragrant tea that is appreciated by most people at first taste. My only objection to this brew is that the taste seems to linger about for hours and finally becomes a bit too much of a good thing.

Pennyroyal.   Oswego Tea.

Another Revolutionary beverage that we should know better is strawberry leaf tea. I long suspected that this good tea had some special health-giving properties, for my Pennsylvania Dutch neighbors trust it to cure many ills, so I took some leaves to Pennsylvania State University and had them tested. In six samples tested, they yielded an average of 229 milligrams of vitamin C to each 100 grams of leaves—and that is very rich indeed. Fresh, green leaves can be picked the year around, and strawberry leaf tea must have protected many an otherwise poorly fed Revolutionary soldier. I use the fresh leaves to make a tea, or watery extract, which is very palatable when flavored with a little lemon and sweetened with honey.

A familiar backwoods tea of the Revolutionary period was made of wintergreen or teaberry leaves. This little plant familiar to acid soils must be freshly picked, for it loses flavor on drying. Don't be afraid to use plenty; fill the pot half full of leaves, pour on boiling water, and let it steep for five minutes. A delightful beverage, it has the familiar wintergreen flavor that is loved by old and young. It is my favorite camp beverage.

For sheer luxury there is no drink that equals the sweet, fragrant tea made of basswood blossoms. Linden blossom tea had long been appreciated in France, both as a home remedy for many minor ills and as a palatable table drink. It may have been the French soldiers who helped us win the Revolutionary War who first introduced Americans to this fine tea. When they saw that the American basswood was almost identical to the European linden, and discovered that its blossoms were even sweeter and more fragrant than the ones they remembered, they probably dried some of the flowers and made tea, which they found to be actually better than the linden tea sold in fine French restaurants. The blossoms should be dried indoors, and the tea is made the same as Oriental tea. It needs little or no sugar, for the evaporated nectar sweetens it with its own natural sugar.

Why not try a few of these native American teas? They are interesting, they are economical, they are educational, they are delicious, they are healthful, and—above all—they are patriotic.

20. Out of the Mailbag

AMONG the joys my writing has brought me are letters from readers all over the world with whom I enjoy corresponding. Some want further amplification of a subject I have mentioned, some have questions about things not mentioned, and many contain solid-gold nuggets of information that I value very highly. The teacher is taught by his students; the writer is instructed by his readers. Some point out errors I have made, while some volunteer additional facts about a subject, and I am grateful to both, for they are making me a better naturalist. I have found readers' letters a far better course in natural history than any I took at my university.

Gastronomically I have profited immensely from the mailbag, for readers have been generous in sharing their wild-food recipes. These recipes are not just buried in my files, but actually are tried. They range from little tea sandwiches to culinary creations that would make the reputation of a good chef.

One reader, for instance, recommends the unlikely combination of cooked pigweed or lamb's quarters with cream cheese and wild blackberry jam as a sandwich filling between little rounds of whole-wheat bread. It sounds gruesome, but tastes perfectly delightful. Another gives a recipe for cream of spring soup that uses half a dozen different wild plants, including wild asparagus, wild watercress, sheep sorrel, morel mushrooms, and wild chervil, and turns out to be one of the most delicious soups I have ever tasted. Still another sent directions for making a marvelous Chinese dish from day-lily buds, rock lichens, and dried mushrooms. On a simpler scale a woman of the mid-South sends along her recipe for wild persimmon-hickory-nut pudding —a soft, creamy concoction that literally melts in the mouth.

I was also sent a recipe for a "protein bar," which a reader's father used for emergency food while hiking. Just blend to your own taste rolled oats, raisins, pitted dates, chopped nuts of any kind that strikes your fancy, chocolate (or carob) bits, and any dried fruit you like, spread all in a shallow pan, then pour freshly rendered very hot suet over it until covered. Before it hardens, cut into bar shapes; then, when it is cold, break it apart and wrap each bar in aluminum foil.

Often letters are sheer eruptions of exuberance about nature and wild foods, bubbling over with the joy of living in intimacy with a newly discovered fellow spirit who understands their enthusiasm.

One reader told me that he has noticed that mosquito larvae are never found in swamps or other standing water in which calamus is growing. This could be of major importance. A non-poisonous method of mosquito control is just what we are looking for. Maybe that very fragrant plant is repulsive to some insects. I think I'll make a water extract of calamus roots and plants, and try spraying it on my garden this season. This is the water plant, *Acorus calamus,* which was strewn on the floors of churches back in the middle ages to make them smell sweet. It also has a high reputation as a medicinal herb, and our informant says that for three years he chewed a small piece of calamus root every day, and during that time never had a cold.

I have heard from hundreds of clever foragers who are enjoying nature's bounty right now, often saving money on gro-

ceries in the process, even on the outskirts of highly industri-
alized and overcivilized metropolitan areas. One is from a pair
of rural hippies who are living a sort of Garden of Eden existence in California on an income of $75 a month. There is an-
other couple who spend their summers in a remote cabin in
British Columbia. They carry in food but live off the land so
completely that they usually have to carry the same food out in
the fall. Hundreds of others, like me, mix their wild food with
civilized fare and have the best of both worlds.

Sometimes the mail brings gifts, rather than exchanges of
ideas, and sometimes it carries them out from our farmhouse to
our friends in far places. Last June in the old orchard on our
place, the ground was so covered with wild strawberries that
they looked like a red carpet in places. I gathered them by the
gallon, and discovered a new way to make wild strawberry jam.
Wild strawberries can be picked very swiftly if one takes them
caps and all, but it takes twice as long to remove the caps as it
does to pick the berries. However, I found that when they are
run though a food mill (such as the Foley), the caps are kept
inside and one gets pure strawberry pulp from which to make
jam. With this speedup I made more than a hundred jars of this
delicious concoction, far more than we could use. Lots of them
have gone for gifts to bring a taste of June during winter
blizzards.

But inspired gifts do not have to be something to eat. Last
Christmas a friend appeared with a bag of pine cones. He had
gathered a great many from the forest nearby, soaked them in a
strong solution of copperas and salt, then dried them and packed
them in decorative bags as gifts. When one of these cones is
tossed into the fireplace it makes the whole fire flame in beautiful
reds, blues, greens, and purples. Throughout the holiday season,
as each cone gave up its beauty, we thought of this friend with
gratitude and closeness.

Up the mountain from where I live a road was widened, destroying a beautiful clump of white birch. I mourned their pass-

ing but determined they should live again in another way. I took the small trunks to my workshop and planed each one smooth on one side, leaving the rest of the white bark intact. Then I sawed each little trunk into six- to ten-inch sections, set them on the planed bases, and drilled holes the right size for candles in the tops. Fitted with red candles and with a bit of red-berried green holly stapled to the white bark, these became beautiful candlesticks for Christmas giving that will last a lifetime; with new greenery fastened on and new candles, they will spread cheer for many holidays to come.

Such gifts carry another message. They say plainer than words that you have been thinking of the receiver more often than just at the last-minute holiday buying rush. If nature's bounty takes care of your Christmas list, you actually can start "shopping" the out-of-doors for next year's gifts the day after Christmas! All year long, as you enjoy the environment around you, gather the makings for what those you care about might like to have at Christmas, and prepare your gifts as you go along. When you give part of nature to someone else who loves her, too, your gift is in true harmony with the spirit of Christmas.

21. On Eating Seaweeds

A WEED-EATER'S experience is incomplete until he has learned to eat seaweeds. I've just returned from a week at the shore, and I am literally full of my subject and getting fuller all the time as I chew on a cud of dulse while I write. Dulse is a reddish seaweed known as *Rhodymenia palmata* to the botanist. I gathered my supply from a rocky tidepool in Maine and dried it in the sun. I chew it slowly, gently, and cautiously, so it won't disintegrate too quickly.

At first taste, dulse has a salty sea flavor, relished by many. But if chewed long and carefully, it gradually becomes permeated with a delightful sweet richness that greatly enhances one's enjoyment. A chemist friend tells me that this is due to the conversion of other carbohydrates into sugar by the diastase in the saliva. All I know is that the longer you chew on a bite of dulse, the better it tastes.

Dulse must be dried before it is edible. Fresh from the tidepool, it is tough and tasteless, giving the sensation of chewing on a salted rubber band. All that is necessary to tenderize and flavor it is a drying in the sun. On clear hot days I have dried dulse to edibility in six hours. One rainy day when I craved

Dulse.

some, I put a little in an openwork onion bag and dried it an hour in the automatic clothes dryer. Dulse does not become brittle and crumbly when dried, but remains springy and flexible.

Most dulse is consumed by merely putting a wad of the dried fronds in the mouth and chewing on it tenderly, lovingly, and leisurely. Almost unknown in the United States, this very healthful food has long been appreciated in Ireland, on the west coast of Scotland, and in the Maritime Provinces of Canada.

In the Mediterranean countries, dulse is used in cooked dishes. I wondered if I could combine New England cooking with Mediterranean cuisine and make a dulse chowder. I took four slices of bacon and one large chopped onion and fried them together until the onion was golden yellow and translucent. Next I added two cups of diced potatoes and one ounce of dried, shredded dulse, covered all with water, and boiled until the potatoes were tender. Then I poured in one quart of milk and added one teaspoon of monosodium glutamate and a quarter-teaspoon of freshly ground black pepper. While heating this to a simmer, I blended one tablespoon of flour in ¼ cup of milk until it was a smooth paste, then stirred this into the chowder and kept stirring until it thickened slightly. I didn't allow the chowder to boil after adding the milk, but did allow it to simmer about ten minutes to remove the raw taste from the thickening. I served this hot with crackers and a tossed watercress salad. My wife and I made a whole meal of it, and we agreed that we had often dined worse.

Although dulse is my favorite, it is not the only seaweed I have been eating during this last week. The same tidepool that yielded the dulse proved to be a little health-food store as far as seaweed products were concerned. Most conspicuous of these treasures were edible kelp (*Alaria esculenta*) which I found flopping in the surge when the mighty tides of Maine were at their lowest ebb. This is a big plant, with a short stem and a single main frond about six inches wide and one to ten feet long, olive-green in color, and having ruffled edges and a conspicuous midrib. Its little fronds are tongue-shaped, about three inches wide and six inches long.

I collected a quantity of this kelp, dried it on the rocks for a day, then finished it up in the clothes dryer. I am no stranger to this food, for I learned to eat it years ago at the homes of my Japanese friends in Hawaii. They called it *oboru kombu*, and used it in many ways. One of the best is a sort of instant soup called *suimono*. Simply put two tablespoons shredded *oboru kombu* and two teaspoons soy sauce in a bowl, cover with boiling water, let stand covered a few minutes, then eat. Another good Japanese dish made with this dried kelp is called *konbu-maki nigiri*. This is a sort of rice sandwich made by wrapping *oboru kombu* around cooked rice that has been seasoned with soy sauce and a little hot mustard. It can also be added to stews, goulashes, and noodle dishes.

Another fine seaweed in my tidepool was laver, a food that's

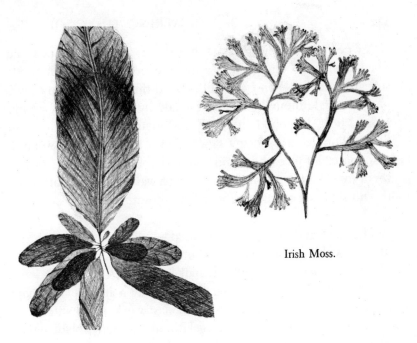

Irish Moss.

Edible Kelp.

also much appreciated by the Japanese. Those living in this country import quantities from Japan, not realizing that the same plant is plentiful on both our coasts. It looks a lot like dulse, but is far thinner, with a filmy, elastic texture and a smooth, satiny sheen. In Japan there are seaweed farms in shallow coastal waters where this seaweed is raised commercially. Farmers merely put down bundles of bamboo to furnish a foothold for the seaweed, and periodically lift them up to harvest the crops.

Laver is treated just like dulse, but being much thinner, it dries more quickly. I made a pretty good soup from it by boiling ½ cup of shredded, dried laver in two cups water until tender, which takes only a few minutes. Then I added one 10½-ounce can of beef consommé and the juice of half a lemon. Reheating just to boiling, I served it with a twist of lemon in each bowl.

An even better dish was stuffed laver fronds. I dipped the dried laver into boiling water a few seconds to make the fronds soft and pliable. Then I carefully spread them out, and on each I placed a little mound of stuffing made by combining ¼ pound ground beef, ¼ pound chopped mushrooms, one medium onion finely chopped, a little soy sauce, and a teaspoon monosodium glutamate. I rolled the fronds around this stuffing and stacked them in a steamer, poured two cups of water into the bottom of it, and steamed them for about fifty minutes. These were really good.

The sides and bottom of my tidepool were carpeted with still another edible seaweed, Irish moss, known to botanists as *Chrondus crispus*. Although it makes a dense carpet that looks like moss while it is growing, this is really a lichen. You have probably eaten Irish moss during the last week, for it enters into the manufacture of ice cream, gelatin-like desserts, blancmange, and beer. Individual plants are three to six inches high and about the same width, flattened, freely forking and reforking until the terminal lobes are many and crowded. Color ranges through olive-green to red, purple, and almost black. The Irish moss of the market is pallid white or cream-colored, but that is because it's bleached in the sun before being sold.

I tried a blancmange (gelatin-milk dessert) with Irish moss fresh from the shore, and it worked perfectly. I merely put a cupful of moss in a piece of cheesecloth and tied it up, then dropped it into two quarts of milk in the top of a double boiler. This was cooked over boiling water for about thirty minutes.

I found it necessary to press the bag and stir the milk frequently, for the gelatinous material from the Irish moss tended to coagulate outside the bag. After a half-hour's steeping, I gave the bag a final squeeze, the milk a final stir, and discarded the spent moss. Then I added ¾ cup raw sugar and a pinch of salt to the milk and allowed it to partly cool. When it began to thicken, I filled it with a quart of freshly picked wild strawberries, poured the blancmange into a mold, and put it in the refrigerator. By evening it was beautifully jelled, with no rubberiness whatever, and it went down as smoothly as a pleasant dream.

I dried a supply to bring home with me. Irish moss, unlike most other seaweeds, doesn't get tender as it dries, it gets tougher. When thoroughly dried, it is stiff and almost hornlike. This dried seaweed still makes excellent jellied fruit desserts, blancmange, puddings, and aspics.

Why bother to eat seaweeds? For centuries, people in various parts of the world have been eating seaweeds for no other reason than because they liked them, enjoyed the taste, and recognized them as nourishing food. The other reason is minerals. The sea is the great repository of all the vital minerals needed by the human body to maintain glowing health, and these minerals are delivered to you in organic form in seaweeds. The introduction of dulse-chewing and seaweed eating to all parts of the country would be a tremendous contribution to public health. All mineral-deficiency diseases would automatically disappear. Goiter would be unknown, and millions would enjoy greater health. The plants are rich in organic iodine and potassium, and give all the trace minerals—known and unknown—that the body needs.

Not only are seaweeds valuable for their mineral content— they furnish tangy taste thrills that fairly shout of the sea. They're also good nourishing foods in other ways, too, containing large amounts of assimilable proteins, carbohydrates, and even some fats.

Ever since Dr. Jarvis wrote his excellent book on *Vermont Folk Medicine*, the sales of kelp have been booming. But this is mainly powdered kelp, in capsules, and therefore a supplement or "medicine." I much prefer eating to taking medicine and find it far more pleasant to get these rare minerals in delicious vegetables and soup dishes than to take countless capsules. As Hippocrates, father of medicine, once said, "Leave your drugs in the chemist's pot if you cannot cure the patient with food."

Now, please don't write and ask me to share my supply of

seaweeds with you. The few pounds I gathered last week won't go around among all my readers. If you can't make a trip to the seashore to gather your own, then try buying *oboru kombu* and red laver at your Oriental grocer's or health-food store. Irish moss can be bought in many supermarkets. You can buy dulse and most other seaweed products by mail from Walnut Acres, Penn's Creek, Pa. And don't write and ask me for seaweed seeds. Seaweed doesn't produce seeds!

22. A Salute to Autumn

I CAN'T abide poets who compose such dirges to autumn as, "The melancholy days are come, the saddest of the year." Drat William Cullen Bryant and all his ilk! Anyone who truly loves nature knows that what Bryant calls "The Death of the Flowers" is no death at all, but a fruition and a fulfillment without which flowers would be a meaningless ornament with no real beauty at all.

The succession of beauty through the season has sunk into my soul until I can see it in the plucking of a ripe apple, smell its fragrance in the aroma, and taste its nectar in each crunchy, juicy bite. I can remove the seeds from the core and thrill to the miracle that these apparently lifeless brown pips contain within them the potentiality of future apple trees bearing blossoms and fruit and seeds, which could produce countless more trees and blossoms—a continuity of life that will go on through all future time.

William Blake, a poet more to my liking, must have seen some such vision when he wrote, "Hold Infinity in the palm of your hand/And eternity in an hour." To me those brown apple seeds are never a dreary obituary to dead apple blossoms, but are a promise and a proof of the flowers' immortality. What is so sad about that?

With my preference for wild foods, I gather nuts each fall directly from God's nut orchard. The wild nuts that find most favor in my section are hickory, black walnuts, butternuts, and wild hazelnuts—and all four seem to be bearing a bumper crop this year.

The black walnut (*Juglans nigra*) is probably the most widely distributed and most abundant of our wild nuts. Millions of bushels are left to rot, sprout, or be eaten by squirrels every year. In gathering black walnuts I usually wear a pair of heavy boots and grind each fallen nut under my heel to remove the husk before picking it up. Wear a plastic glove while gathering them, or you will get a stain on your hands that is almost impossible to remove. I put the freshly husked nuts into a fruit basket, then dry them in my cellar near the furnace.

In the last few years I have discovered an even easier way to acquire my supply of black walnuts. When fall fills the forest with riotous colors, I must be out driving, for I am a glutton for such beauty—so I combine my two pleasures by filling my eyes with feasts of beauty and filling my cellar with wild nuts. At that time the black walnuts have all fallen from the trees, and since many of the best walnut trees overhang the country roads on which I drive, the roadsides are lined with nuts that have already been husked by being run over by the tires of passing traffic. The autumn sun has dried them until they are already stainproof, and all I have to do is come along and claim them.

I was once singing the praises of the black walnut as an ingredient in fudge, cakes, and cookies when a woman who is an excellent cook said, "You don't have to convince me that black walnuts are good—all you have to do is tell me how to get them out of those awful shells." That is a problem, and I don't guarantee to make the shelling of black walnuts easy, but I have found that it gets progressively easier with practice. If you stand the nut pointed end up on a solid surface and hit it a sharp blow

Butternut.

with a hammer, it will crack into two halves. Stand each half, again pointed end up, and strike it again, and you will have broken it into quarters. Strike each quarter again on the pointed end, and it will break crosswise into eighths this time—at which point the nutmeats will fall out.

When the nuts are well dried, I have been able to empty shell after shell completely without resorting to a nutpick. I find these eighths of walnut meat just the right size without further chopping, to include in cakes, muffins, or fruit-nut breads, and the delicious flavor will survive even prolonged baking. Shelled nuts can be sealed in a plastic bag and stored in the freezer. A year later they will taste as fresh and sweet as the day they were shelled.

The butternut is a close relative of the black walnut, but is a slightly smaller tree, with a lighter-colored bark and oblong nuts borne in clusters of two to five. Harvesting and husking is much the same task as with the black walnut. The shell is very hard and horny, but once it is broken the kernel is comparatively easy to separate. It is sweet and delicious and very oily. This nut is for those who must have the perfect ingredient for cakes, cookies, and other baked goods that call for nuts.

Many people consider the hickory nut the finest of our wild nuts. There are a number of species bearing good nuts growing from New England to Minnesota and south to Florida and Texas. A few species bear nuts too bitter and acrid to eat, but none are harmful. My favorite is the shagbark (*Carya ovata*), which makes up for its comparatively small size by being thin-shelled and having an exceptionally sweet and delicious kernel.

The husk on a hickory obligingly opens and lets the husked nuts fall to the ground, so harvesting is merely a matter of picking them up from under the tree. Select for raiding the hickories that grow in pastures, along fencerows, or otherwise away from other trees. Those that grow among other trees usually produce scant crops of nuts, and these are taken by the squirrels as fast as they ripen.

I can give you a secret for shelling hickory nuts. Put the unshelled nuts in the deep freeze for a day, then remove a few handfuls at a time and shell them while they are still frozen and brittle. The nuts are narrower one way than the other, so hold them up edgewise and strike each a sharp blow with the hammer, just hard enough to crack the shell well without smashing the kernel. Cracked this way, many entire halves can be removed, while the others usually come out in quarters. These nuts are excellent for use in baked goods, as well as being one of our finest for just eating as they are shelled.

The well-known pecan is really only one species of hickory, and this excellent nut grows wild over a large range extending from Indiana through Illinois, southern Iowa, Kansas, and south to Alabama and Texas. I was practically weaned on wild pecans in my east Texas home. Surely I don't have to tell any forager worth his salt to gather all he can find.

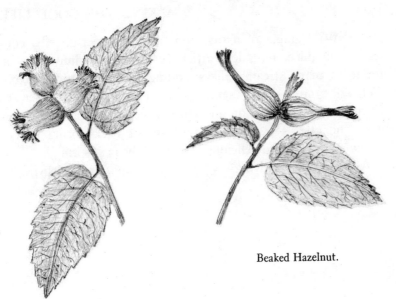

Beaked Hazelnut.

Hazelnut.

Another wild nut that can easily be overlooked is the hazelnut that grows on small bushes by so many roadsides. I was amazed to find that few of my neighbors are even aware that hazelnuts grow in the area where I live, though I know thicket after thicket of these sweet little nuts. The supply *is* limited, so I'm not about to enlighten them. These nuts ripen in late August but hang onto the bushes until late fall—unless I or some other wild animal happens by. They are small, round, sweet, and easily shelled, with all the goodness of cultivated filberts, if not more. There is a rumor that these nuts are excellent to cook with, but I seem unable to get them from the shell into any container besides my mouth.

Do you wonder why I don't find autumn depressing? This is harvest time for much besides the nuts, and is the season when undomesticated nature offers some of her finest treasures. I do love the wild persimmon's little golden globes of sugary goodness, and this is the time of the year when they are in their prime. Wild grapes of many kinds make wonderful jelly, conserve, and juice. Jerusalem artichokes and groundnuts can be found in many stream valleys, adding welcome variety to my diet. The ground cherry makes the finest jam this side of heaven. Even the lowly dandelion and chicory lose their summer bitterness, and after a few freezes they sprout back during Indian summer as sweet and delicious as they will be next spring.

Autumn time of dying? Never! It is a time for royal living.

23. Wild Winter Vitamins

A SCORBIC acid deficiency has probably killed more people than all the wars of history, and the sad part is that nearly all these deaths could have been prevented. Scurvy, which is no more than the multiple symptoms of acute ascorbic acid deficiency—a lack of vitamin C—was a scourge every year in the late winter and early spring for hundreds of years, in both Northern Europe and young America. Many died each year as a direct result of scurvy, and a great many more died of infections from which they could have recovered had they been amply supplied with vitamin C to let their bodies put up a fair fight against disease.

The reason for all this suffering and death was that before the development of canning and freezing, people tended to live during the winter almost entirely on dried or salted foods, thereby getting little or no vitamin C in their diets at that time of the year. Soldiers in the field and sailors at sea, living on these vitaminless foods at all times of year, were the hardest hit. Captain Cook did not make his greatest contribution to mankind by discovering Hawaii, or by exploring the South Seas, but by his discovery that men long at sea could be protected from scurvy by feeding them fresh fruit and vegetables at every opportunity, and giving them lime juice and sauerkraut when fresh produce was unobtainable. Of course Captain Cook never heard of vitamin C—but he made good use of it, nevertheless.

Long before Captain Cook, a few people had begun to suspect that there was some connection between scurvy and the absence of fresh fruit and vegetables in the diet. The guelder rose, or European high-bush cranberry (*Viburnum opulus*), bears bountiful clusters of somewhat bitter and very sour fruit which will hang on the shrub throughout the winter. Chaucer, the fourteenth-century poet, mentions this as a healer of scurvy. He calls the fruit "gaitre berries," lists them among the plants that "shal be for your hele," and recommends that you "picke him right as they grow and eat hem in"—an excellent way to take full advantage of this berry's not inconsiderable vitamin C content.

I had this berry analyzed for ascorbic acid at Penn State University and they found that it contained about 100 milligrams of this important vitamin per 100 grams of fruit, a rich yield. The berry still grows, not only in England but over here, and our American variety is far more palatable than the kind that grows abroad, making it a pleasure to "eat hem in." Had northern Europeans and early Americans taken advantage of this winter fruit, much suffering and death would have been prevented.

One doesn't need high-bush cranberries, however, to prevent scurvy in winter. It is surprising how many things stay green all winter—and nearly every green thing contains at least a little vitamin C. Even pine needles contain enough vitamin C to prevent scurvy if used regularly. Ascorbic acid is water-soluble, so a watery extract of any material containing it will serve as a vitamin drink. To get the maximum amount from such substances as green pine needles, chop them fine, cover with boiling water, and let them steep until the next day. A glassful of this piny drink would at least prevent the worst deficiency symptoms.

Wild Rose Hips.

Wild rose hips also hang on the bush all winter, and these can furnish a real vitamin concentrate. Rose fruits are probably nature's richest source of ascorbic acid in the Intemperate Zone. A cupful of pared rose hips will furnish as much vitamin C as ten to twelve dozen oranges. You don't have to just "eat hem in" straight from the bush, either, although I have often done that. You can pick the hips and make a good jam. Formerly I made this jam in the blender—really an easy way to do it—but the product looks too much like orange-colored mud to suit my fancy. Now I gather the rose hips, remove the stem and blossom ends with a sharp knife, then make a slit down each side of the hip and remove the seeds. I chop the seedless hips rather coarsely.

When I have two cups of prepared hips ready, I add three cups of raw sugar and the juice of one lemon and stir, stir, stir—until the sugar is dissolved. Then I put one package of powdered commercial pectin in 3¾ cup water, bring it to a rolling boil, and boil hard for one minute. I then stir this quickly but thoroughly into the sweetened rose hips and quickly pour it into ½-pint glass jars and seal with dome lids. Since it is uncooked, nearly all the vitamin C content is preserved, but also because it is uncooked, it won't keep on the shelf. It will keep very well in the refrigerator for a month. If you intend to hold it longer than that, store it in the freezer. A tablespoonful of this delicious jam will easily give you your daily minimum requirements of vitamin C. Isn't that better than taking a pill?

Another plant that I have explored for its vitamin C content is ground ivy (*Glechoma hederacea*), a very small round-leaved plant of the mint family that grows everywhere here and all over Europe. This is another plant that can be gathered green all year round. In reading old herbals, I found it recommended for the treatment of scurvy and "painter's colic"—an old term used for some of the symptoms of lead poisoning. A doctor friend tells me that the modern treatment for this poisoning is to give massive doses of vitamin C, for the lead combines with ascorbic acid before being eliminated from the body. In the absence of this vitamin, it becomes a very dangerous, cumulative poison. Even such tiny doses as one gets from breathing modern-day exhaust-polluted air containing lead (used as an additive in gasoline) can build up to dangerous levels unless the body is amply supplied with ascorbic acid.

The Food and Nutrition Lab at Penn State University found

that ground ivy contains about 55 milligrams of ascorbic acid per 100 grams of the whole herb. This is not a particularly rich yield, but the fact that this plant was available at the time of year that scurvy was at its worst made it invaluable in treating this illness. Of course, it was the same vitamin C that made this plant valuable in treating painter's colic.

Unfortunately, many of the old herbalists thought the virtue of this herb lay in some drug it contained, so they dried it, prepared an extract from it, or distilled it, and used these products in treating the illnesses they had administered the fresh herb for previously. Of course they had processed the ascorbic acid right out of the plant—and it no longer cured. This caused many doctors to reject the plant altogether.

The same thing has happened again and again in herbal medicine. A plant appeared to have almost miraculous healing powers. It cured dozens of "diseases." Then along came a doctor who decided to give it an exhaustive test. He couldn't be bothered to go out and gather fresh herbs every day, so he accumulated a big pile of the dried herb, or a few jugs of some kind of extract from it, and then found these useless in treating the diseases this plant was supposed to cure. He promptly pronounced it worthless. Of course, what happened is that the so-called "diseases" the herb had formerly been curing were really acute vitamin deficiencies alleviated by the vitamin content of the fresh herb. It was food, not drugs, that was effecting the cures. Naturally, when the plant was used in a form that no longer contained the vitamins, it was worthless.

My favorite winter vitamin source is the plant called winter cress, or yellow rocket, which is often called "wild mustard" by local farmers in the area. It is a member of the mustard family, but I prefer to reserve the term "mustard" for the Brassicas, or garden mustards, also often found wild. While winter cress has lobed leaves like mustard, they are bright and shiny, not hairy like mustard leaves. They are also thicker and fleshier, and when eaten lack the pungency one associates with mustard.

Winter Cress.

I have gathered winter cress every month of the year. From New York southward it brightens up and grows during every warm spell in winter. It gained its botanical name, *Barbarea*, because it was green and edible on Saint Barbara's day, December 4th. Not only is it obtainable in winter, it is actually much better to eat then, becoming bitter in summer.

Winter cress is at its best after the first hard freeze in autumn until the last frost of spring. Cooked as one would boil cabbage or spinach and served with a garnish of crisp, crumbled bacon, there are few vegetables that equal it for flavor. It is often found growing as a field or garden weed. In any case, if you'd eat the weed and ignore the crop, without doubt you'd be getting more nutrition.

I can find no record that winter cress had ever been explored for vitamin content until I took it to the labs at Penn State. It turned out to be a nutritional giant! Three tests gave us an average of 152 milligrams of ascorbic acid per 100 grams of leaves, and 5067 International units of vitamin A per 100 grams. This is more vitamin C than is found in any garden vegetable listed in Agriculture Handbook No. 8, the official U.S. publication on the Composition of Foods, and it rates very high in vitamin A.

I also discovered one of the finest sources of wild winter vitamins through observing my Pennsylvania Dutch neighbors. An old, wild orchard on my place is carpeted with wild strawberries. One winter day I looked out my study window and saw a neighbor boy picking something from the ground. Naturally I wanted to know what he was finding in the dead of winter that was valuable enough to go to all that trouble to gather. Quickly I bundled and booted up and joined him. He was gathering wild strawberry leaves, which stay green all winter—even under the snow. He said his mother had sent him out to gather these leaves to make strawberry leaf tea.

I went home with him and asked his mother why she was so anxious to make this tea that she would send her son out in the snow to gather the leaves. She said, "When I start feeling rundown and no-good, and my gums get soft, and even a tiny scratch makes a sore that won't heal—then I know it's time for me to drink some green strawberry leaf tea." I was amazed. This country woman, who didn't know vitamin C from vitamin Z, had just listed a number of acute ascorbic acid deficiency symptoms and was apparently applying the proper remedy. Not only that, her method of making the tea extracted the maximum amount of vitamins from the leaves. She poured boiling water over the leaves, covered the pot, and let it set until the next day, then drank it cold while preparing another supply for the following day.

At that time I didn't know how much vitamin C strawberry leaves contained—nor even if they contained any at all—and as far as I could determine, neither did anyone else. I advised the woman to eat winter cress, as well, and feed it to her family as soon as it could be obtained.

As soon as the snow melted off, I gathered a plastic bag full of wild strawberry leaves and headed for Penn State. They ran three separate tests for ascorbic acid content and obtained an average of 229 milligrams of this vitamin per 100 grams of leaves—such an amazing amount that they refused to believe it. The lab technician practically accused me of adding ascorbic acid to my sample. She found this quantity of vitamin C so unbelievable that she went out and gathered a new supply of wild strawberry leaves herself to prove me wrong. However, when the new supply yielded an even higher quantity of ascorbic acid, she reluctantly admitted that strawberry leaves were really an excellent source of vitamin C, and that the country people who have been treating ascorbic acid deficiency with green strawberry leaf tea knew what they were about.

It saddens me to think of all the illness and death caused by ascorbic acid deficiency among the early settlers of this country. It could all have been prevented had they known which of the many wild winter plants to add to their diet. At least I know I will never die of scurvy as long as nature keeps offering such a wide assortment of free vitamin pills throughout the year.

24. Wild Health Foods

WHILE talking to an assembly at an elementary school about wild foods, I was asked a theological question. One little boy, who was particularly horrified at the idea of eating weeds, asked, "If God had intended us to eat these plants, wouldn't he have them growing in fields or gardens, rather than just growing wild?" When I explained that God had never put any plants in neat orderly rows in fields and gardens, but had just scattered them through nature, and it had been man who domesticated those he needed, the boy was satisfied, but I wasn't.

Nature, which is God's most active and visible hand, does seem to be thrusting certain plants at us, and we seem to be just as determinedly thrusting them away. Some of the very best wild plants—best both in flavor and nutritional composition—do grow in gardens and fields. They snuggle right up to our food plants and grow there stubbornly, persistently, and despite all our efforts to eradicate them. When I walk into my organic garden and see these plants, self-sown and self-tended, growing next to the food plants I'm trying to grow there, they seem to be saying to me, "Look at us. You must have come here searching for food. Why not take advantage of the fine flavors and healthful nutrition we can offer?"

Probably the three most common garden weeds in this country—ones that grow from border to border and coast to coast—are (1) green amaranth (*Amaranthus retroflexus*), sometimes called "rough pigweed," (2) lamb's quarters (*Chenopodium album*), sometimes called "smooth pigweed," or "white goosefoot," which is a literal translation of its Latin name, and (3) purslane or "pusley" (*Portulaca oleracea*), sometimes called "low pigweed," a sprawling, ground-hugging, fat-leaved, succulent-stemmed rampant growing plant.

Green amaranth is distantly related to beets and is occasionally called "wild beet." Pull one up, and you see that the root is red, like an undeveloped beet. The greens, although not very strongly flavored, are pretty good food if gathered from young plants. They are mild, some say tasteless, but excellent to mix with strongly flavored, pungent potherbs, such as marsh marigold (*Caltha palustris*) or wild mustard, to bring their strong flavors down to palatable levels.

Let's see how green amaranth stacks up against beet greens nutritionally. For these comparisons I will look at protein, iron, vitamin A, and vitamin C. This is not to downgrade any other constituents, nor to elevate the importance of these four, but merely because they are important nutrients and because I happen to have data on them.

	Protein	Iron	Vitamin A	Vitamin C
Amaranth greens	3.5	3.9	6100	80
Beet greens	2.2	3.3	6100	20

In all the tables protein is given in grams per 100 grams, iron and vitamin C are both in milligrams per 100 grams, and vitamin A is given in International Units per 100 grams. Two things stand out here. One is that beet greens make a very good health food, and the other is that amaranth greens are even better.

How about lamb's quarters, the most cosmopolitan weed of

Amaranth.

them all? It is closely related to spinach and Swiss chard, and of course it is also related to beets, and therefore related to green amaranth. Let's look at its analysis.

	Protein	Iron	Vitamin A	Vitamin C
Lamb's quarters	4.2	1.2	11600	80
Spinach	3.2	3.1	8100	51
Swiss chard	2.4	3.2	6500	32

The message is clear. Spinach is a little better food than Swiss chard, though Swiss chard is very good, and lamb's quarters is far better than either, coming out ahead in every department except iron content.

And speaking of iron, look at the lowly purslane. This plant has no domestic counterpart with which to compare it, but purslane itself has long been a domesticated garden plant in

many countries, with horticultural varieties that stand up instead
of sprawling in the sand. I can't understand why purslane never
became a popular vegetable in this country, for it can be eaten
raw or cooked and is an excellent health food.

	Protein	Iron	Vitamin A	Vitamin C
Purslane	1.7	3.5	2500	25

That huge iron content is even more surprising when one
discovers that purslane is about 93 percent water. Its 3.5 milligrams of iron per 100 grams of purslane make it richer in iron
than any domestic vegetable except parsley, which has a
whopping 6.1 milligrams per 100 grams. Did you ever eat 100
grams of parsley, which is about 3.5 ounces or nearly a quarter-
pound, at one meal? I never did, but I can easily eat a half-
pound of purslane either cut into a tossed salad or wilted in the
frying pan with some bacon.

Let's go outside the vegetable garden and see what other
plants seem to be trying to thrust themselves on our attention.
Probably the most common lawn weed throughout the world is
the dandelion. Millions are spent each year on herbicides in a
vain attempt to eradicate this really pretty little flower. I think it
must be the persistence of the dandelion that annoys us; it is
certainly not its appearance. It simply refuses to be banished and
keeps insisting that we pay attention to it. What is it trying to tell
us?

Apparently it has got its message across several times in history. Its Latin name is *Taraxacum officinale*, which can be
roughly translated, "the official remedy for disorders," and
ancient books of herbal medicines list dozens of illnesses for
which the specific treatment is dandelion in some form. It could
cetainly remedy any disorder caused by a deficiency of vitamin
A. The nearest relatives of the wild dandelion that we commonly
raise in our vegetable gardens are endive and lettuce. Let's stack
them up over one another and see where we come out.

	Protein	Iron	Vitamin A	Vitamin C
Dandelion	2.7	3.1	14000	35
Endive	1.7	1.7	3300	10
Leaf lettuce	1.3	1.4	1900	18
Head lettuce	0.9	0.4	330	6

No question about who is champion here. Endive and leaf lettuce lag far behind the dandelion, and head lettuce isn't even in the running. And don't try to tell me that dandelions are not palatable. Cut off just below the top of the root in the very early spring, before the last frost, and long before the first bloom, with the tough outside leaves peeled away, the tops of all large leaves discarded and with only the heart of the dandelion left, they are good in salads with potatoes, bacon, and vinegar, and boiled and buttered they are one of the finest cooked vegetables I know. After warm weather comes, the dandelion is too bitter to be enjoyed by most people, but the tiny buds that immediately precede the first blooming in spring are the finest vegetable ever eaten, though somewhat tedious to gather. And remember, after the first freeze in the fall, during Indian summer, dandelions are again as good as they were in the spring.

What about some of the other weeds that seem to be vying for our attention? Plantain (*Plantago major*) is another lawn weed we are constantly trying to eradicate. This, too, is edible and probably very rich in vitamin A, to judge by its color, and quite likely it is also rich in the other nutrients we are considering, but I can find no record that it was ever explored by a food analyst. Here is a chance for someone with the know-how who has a laboratory available to do a service for us health-food eaters.

I do know people who make a baby food of plantain in their blender. Since the baby appears to thrive on it, I decided it was safe enough for me to try. After the first few trials of plantain in salad and as a plain cooked green, I thought I understood why this family fed it only to a baby too small to protest, and didn't eat it themselves. It has a strong "herby" flavor. However, I

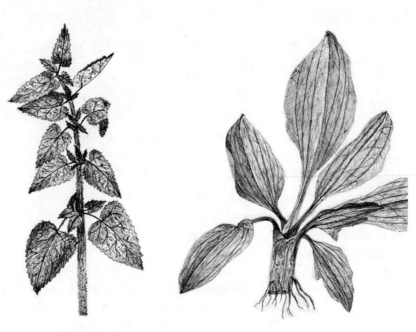

Stinging Nettle.   Common Plantain.

finally made a cream of plantain soup that I think one of the
finest soups that ever graced a table.

Boil about a half-pound of plantain leaves in one can of beef
consommé and one can of water, for thirty minutes. Slice four
green onions thinly, including the green tops, and sauté in two
tablespoons of butter until the white parts turn golden brown.
Sprinkle one tablespoon of flour over the scallions, then add one
cup of the broth from the greens pot, and boil and stir until
smooth. Then pour all back into the plantain pot and boil for
ten minutes more. Rub through a sieve or ricer. This is to purée
everything and to get the tough fiber out of the plantain leaves.
Return the strained soup to low heat and add one cup of light
cream into which one beaten egg yolk has been stirred. Heat and
stir, but do not boil, until it is piping hot, then serve with a
sprinkling of powdered mace. This makes it taste like the very
breath of spring.

Which other wild plants are shouting into our deaf ears? How about that yellow rocket, winter cress, or wild mustard (*Barbarea verna*), which grows so profusely in fields south of New York? It becomes very conspicuous in May when it shows its thousands of cross-shaped yellow blossoms, but by then it is too bitter to eat, so we must learn to recognize it earlier. The hearts of the plants, gathered while nights are still frosty, make one of the finest vegetables I have ever eaten. Cooked or raw, it is a delicacy.

Those stinging nettles that pain our ankles—what are they trying to tell us? Gathered in early spring while still less than a foot high, nettles (*Urtica dioica*) make a palatable vegetable. Use plastic workgloves, for even young nettles can sting fiercely. Take only the tops with the newest, tenderest leaves. Cover the nettle tops with water and stir with a wooden spoon until they are thoroughly washed. Dip them from the wash water with a pair of kitchen tongs and drop into a kettle. Add no water—the few drops that cling to the leaves will be plenty.

Cover the kettle and cook slowly until nettles are as tender as cooked spinach, which takes about ten minutes. Season and serve. Cooking completely removes this plant's stinging abilities—indeed, it converts the very material the nettle uses in its stinger into very good, high-protein food, for the nettle has more protein than any other leafy material known.

	Protein	Iron	Vitamin A	Vitamin C
Yellow rocket	—	—	5067	152
Nettle tops	6.9	—	6566	76

The dashes simply mean nothing is known about how much of these constituents the plant has. I would bet on both these plants being rich in iron. I could find no analysis of either of them, so had an analysis made in the labs of Pennsylvania State University.

What does all this mean? Have we domesticated the wrong plants? I don't think so. One can get all the vitamins and minerals he needs from plants already under cultivation, if they are organically grown and eaten as fresh as possible. So if you wish to, you can safely ignore these shouting plants, and try to eradicate them. I have no fear that your efforts will endanger the species!

I think the proper way to heed what these nutritious plants are saying is to gather the wild ones, save the weeds as we weed our organic gardens, seek out natural plantations, and use them. But don't gather them where herbicides have been sprayed.

However, if I know organic gardeners, they are going to want to control the growth of these nutritious plants, rather than depend on chance wildings. I don't know where you can buy seed for these wild plants. No, I won't gather seeds for you; I have neither the time nor the desire to go into the wild-seed business. I don't know anything about the horticultural requirements of these plants, and I can't give you directions for raising them. In my experience, they raise themselves very well.

Now let me throw out a challenge. Are you really interested in these plants? Are you interested enough to learn to recognize them in the wild? I suggest that you pick them from the wild and cook and eat them before you even consider growing them in your garden. I have purposely picked six common weeds, wild plants that grow in every state. Survey your own area. See how many of these plants already grow there, and how plentifully. Would it be a redundance to plant them in your garden? Ask the botany teacher at your local school how to recognize them— carrying in the plants that you suspect to be the ones. If, after getting thoroughly acquainted with them, you still wish to grow them in your garden, then gather your own seeds, from wild plants going to seed.

If these aggressive wild plants don't grow in your area, there is probably something about the climate or soil that will also prevent them from growing in the garden. If they could grow in your area but don't simply because they have never been introduced there, it would be very poor ecology to introduce such aggressive weeds to become pests to farmers and gardeners. Personally, I love these wild plants as wild plants and haven't the slightest desire to see them domesticated. For my part, they can stay wild, and I will not have to dig, delve, spade, seed, cultivate, water, mulch, and fertilize. I will merely go out and gather them when they are ready to eat. As Emerson said, "A weed is a plant whose virtues we have not yet discovered."

25. Taming Wild Plants

THE fact that a large number of excellent edible wild plants simply refuse to be domesticated surprises many people. They think, "If this plant can survive and bear fruit with no care whatever, then surely it will flourish if I care for it properly." When early French settlers penetrated to the Ohio valley, they found the Indians enjoying the groundnut (*Apios tuberosa*) and immediately took it to France, where they tried to domesticate it. A climbing vine that entwines other vegetation in the wild, it could be accommodated by providing poles for it to climb, as we do with pole beans. However, there were other problems not solved so easily. The groundnut grows in almost marshy, alluvial soil. It will not grow in dry ground, nor will it grow where water stands, but needs rich soil that is continuously damp although not quite watersoaked. Can you duplicate this condition in your garden?

Yet there are ideal places for the groundnut to grow wild along nearly every stream valley. But in the few places that the French found where it would grow, they had trouble. This plant produces strands of tubers connected by string-like roots. However, it does not produce this long string in one year—it is a perennial that links its underground tubers over several years. They grow only an inch or so under the surface of the soil. How do you cultivate such a plant? You can't hoe or plow without damaging the nuts. The French finally gave up and decided to let the groundnut remain a wild plant.

During the first World War a German scientist investigated the common stinging nettle (*Urtica dioica*) with amazing results. He found that this ordinary weed of waste places, fence-rows, and waysides was an excellent food, furnishing vitamins, carbohydrates, and an astounding amount of protein. While domestic animals refused to eat the live plants, they could be dried into an extremely nourishing hay relished by many kinds of livestock. And stalks of the mature plant yielded a fiber that in some ways is superior to flax.

It was immediately decided that this formerly despised weed could be a valuable crop. Seed was given to a number of farmers who agreed to try to raise it. Although they anticipated no trouble in raising a plant that would grow voluntarily without care, not a single one produced a good crop of nettles. Because this plant seemed to grow so easily in the wild, the farmers had assumed that it was not very particular about its growing conditions. They could not have been more wrong.

After these failures, the scientist went back for a closer investigation of the habitats in which the nettles naturally grow. He found that this plant invariably chooses soil far richer than the average German field. The English have a saying, "Plant a fruit tree where nettles grow"—and how right they are. Where nettles grow well you find soil of almost perfect balance in plant nutrients. It is amazing how many of these little perfect spots are found in nature, where patches of nettles flourish.

A great many other wild-food plants are, for one reason or another, not suitable for domestication. But there are some excellent edible wild plants that thrive under the care a gardener can give them. Most organic gardeners know there are horticultural varieties of the common dandelion, chicory, winter

Poke.

cress, salsify, mustard, and many other plants that are also common wild foods.

Domestic varieties of burdock are popular in Japan, while over here it's a common dooryard weed, and in Europe several varieties of purslane, one of the most common garden weeds, have been developed for crop-raising. But we have hardly touched the wild for the treasures it can offer. Let's look at a wild green vegetable that may prove a real garden gem.

Poke (*Phytolacca americana*), also called inkberry, garget, pigeonberry, and other names, is probably the best known and most widely used wild vegetable in this country, with the possible exception of dandelion greens. But few people seem to give even a thought to raising it in their gardens. Maybe that's because most people who like it are country people who live within its wide range and can gather all they want from the wild. Poke, like nettles, revels in rich soil, but is not quite so demanding in this respect. It will grow very well in the average organic garden, and it seems to thrive especially when fertilized with compost or manure.

One can start poke from seed, which means gathering pokeberries in the fall, washing out and drying the seed, then planting them in early spring. The only time I tried this I got a good stand with no trouble. However, this is like starting an asparagus bed from seed. It takes several years before you have a good poke bed, for you cannot use it at all the first year and only very sparingly the second and third years. A much better way is to gather mature roots from the wild, then set out a bed that will come into full production the first year.

Poke grows wild, often in a great abundance, from southern New England to Florida and west to Iowa and Texas. The time to dig roots from wild plants is in the fall, when they are very conspicuous and easily found. The plant grows to six or eight feet high with stout stems an inch or two in diameter, usually with clusters of six to fifteen spreading from the same root. In the autumn these stems turn an attractive purple or lavender color and produce many clusters of berries so dark a purple that they appear black. Our ancestors used the juice of these berries as ink, and one can still see old letters—clear and unfaded— written in pokeberry ink with a quill pen.

The root of a large poke plant may be as big as your thigh and almost as long as your leg. The inside is white and succulent and appears almost edible—but don't try it, for the root of poke is poisonous, containing an alkaloid called *phytolaccin* that is a drastic purgative.

You needn't be too careful and gentle in collecting these roots, though. When one is too long to dig easily, just cut it off a foot or so below the surface and it will grow fine. I have planted many—some with the bottoms chopped off—and they have never failed to grow. Plant roots about two feet apart in your garden. The following April, these will sprout, each one sending up a dozen or so fat shoots looking a bit like stout asparagus with a leafy top. Don't gather them too soon, for the very young shoots are slightly astringent. But when they reach six to twelve inches high, they make a fine vegetable.

Like asparagus, poke can be picked several times, as the mighty root sends up new sprouts if you cut the first ones. However, there is a limit to the number of potential buds on top of that huge root, so after about three cuttings let the plant grow, in order to have a strong root for next year's crop.

Poke is a nutritional giant, being far richer in vitamins and minerals than any of the commonly grown domestic vegetables. Each 100 grams of raw poke contains 2.6 grams of protein and 3.7 grams of carbohydrate, plus 1.7 milligrams of iron, 136 milligrams of vitamin C, 8700 International Units of Vitamin A, and significant amounts of thiamin, riboflavin, and niacin.

Poke can be prepared for the table in several ways. It is most often served as a boiled vegetable. Boil in plenty of water for ten minutes, then drain. This is to remove any stray phytolaccin and prevent astringency. Return the poke to the kettle with very little water, and season with butter or bacon drippings. Slowly simmer for thirty minutes so seasonings can cook through the vegetable, then serve plain, in a cream sauce or covered with hollandaise sauce. Or try covering the cooked sprouts with hot undiluted canned cheese soup.

I know all the health-foods cooks are going to jump all over me about that parboiling and draining, asking why I even mention the nutrients if I am going to pour them down the drain. You do lose some water-soluble vitamins when you drain boiled vegetables, but you don't lose them all. I have before me an analysis of poke raw and poke cooked by being boiled and drained. Vitamin C is reduced from 136 milligrams per 100 grams to 82 milligrams, and the other nutrients are hardly changed at all, being reduced only very slightly as the water content is increased. That 82 milligrams per 100 grams is still richer than any other common garden vegetable. Poke is so rich in nutrients that you can afford to waste some of them.

The leafy tops of poke can be cooked separately, but, unlike spinach, these greens should be thoroughly cooked. Some like to combine them with mustard greens, but they are very good cooked alone. Just follow the directions for cooking sprouts, and you'll have as fine a dish of greens as you ever tasted.

A third dish made from this plant is fried poke. Take the stouter stems, peel and slice them into disks, then roll in corn meal and fry in deep fat. Drain on paper towels, and serve while still hot. This is a favorite method of preparing poke in southern Indiana.

Do not use poke after it begins to bloom, for then the phytolaccin starts appearing throughout the plant. Children should be taught not to eat the berries, as the seeds contain a considerable amount of this strong laxative. The lavender stems in late autumn are beautiful in fall flower arrangements.

26. Taming Wild Fruits

I'VE always been a little impatient with people whose only interest in wild plants was whether or not they could be captured, made to grow in straight rows, and to yield something useful or profitable for their owners. It is this *owner* idea that bugs me. It seems that some people can take no joy in anything unless they can make it their own. Why can't we—at least some of the time—relate to nature in some non-possessive way?

TO A FRIEND

I would not chain a falcon to my wrist,
Nor jail a mockingbird within a cage,
For I can love the free, and not insist
That wildings be reduced to vassalage.
I would not tame the white-tailed doe, nor make
Wild flowers grow in cultivated ground,
They bloom not only for my selfish sake;
Not for my ears alone the songbirds sound.
I cannot own the distant, shining star,
And yet its light is treasured none the less
And you are precious being what you are,
For I can love, and never need possess.

I own you not, and yet my love survives
Though winds of freedom blow between our lives.

Another friend, to whom I have often expounded my philosophy, caught me this spring spreading manure around a wild persimmon tree and ribbed me for being inconsistent. Was I not bringing this tree under cultivation and ordering it to produce fruit for my use? And wasn't I thereby establishing ownership? This accusation caught me by surprise, for I had not a single thought of taking possession of the tree. Last fall it donated many pounds of delicious fruit to my larder. I had reveled all winter in persimmon–hickory-nut bread, persimmon puddings, and persimmon chiffon pies. There is still a satisfying hoard of strained persimmon pulp in my freezer.

It was not covetousness, but gratitude and generosity that were prompting my actions. This tree had greatly added to the joy of my life. What could I do for it? The least I could do was to contribute some plant food in exchange. It then occurred to me that maybe this was the way domestication of food plants started. Some grateful recipient of wild bounty—in trying to deepen his relationship with nature—contributed fertilizer, pruning, weeding, or cultivation to his benefactor, and found that his act had also increased the amount of food the plant would give to him. Such a relationship would not be possessive, but cooperative and mutually beneficial. At this moment the first organic gardener was born.

Despite my own predilection for wild plants, I have nothing against the gardeners, farmers, or orchardists whose main interest is in domestic plants. If they approach their tasks with an attitude of cooperation rather than conquest of nature, then they are also relating in a creative and constructive way. They endeavor to discover what nature wants, and don't try to force her hand with concentrated chemicals and poisonous sprays.

All the food plants on which we depend once came to us from the wild. We tend to think of this domestication process as something that occurred in prehistory, but it is still going on.

It was after Europeans came to this country that the fox grape was developed into the *Concord*, and a number of related varieties. The native red raspberry and the black cap were improved and cultivated. In Maine, wild blueberries were merely protected and encouraged, becoming a semi-domesticated crop on what is called "improved blueberry land." The real domestic blueberries were developed during this century by selecting exceptionally good wild plants and propagating them asexually. This process is still going on through selections of promising blueberry seedlings.

In some areas domestication is barely begun. Maple syrup and maple sugar are still made from the sap of wild maple trees. Some are semi-domesticated to the extent that the wild trees were actually planted and protected from competition of other life forms. But until recently there has been no attempt to improve the sugar maple and develop horticultural varieties despite the fact that few wild plants have shown greater promise of repaying such effort.

The sap from one maple tree may assay as much as nine percent sugar, while the next tree may have as little as one percent. Obviously, a grove of nine percent trees would be much better than a grove of one percent trees. But so far there is no way to predict which sapling or seedling will be the sweeter tree. Will the sweet-sapped trees come true from seed? Can the extra-sweet trees be grafted, budded, layered, or otherwise reproduced, and will the offspring have as sweet sap as did their parents? No one knows. The University of Vermont is now engaged in experiments that may eventually answer some of these questions. The answers won't be here tomorrow, for with each change made, a generation of maple trees must be grown before the result can be known—and that takes time.

At the same time, some native trees can still be considered only partly domesticated. Horticultural varieties of black walnut and hickory nuts are no more than selected exceptional wild trees that have been artificially propagated. Even certain strains of oak are beginning to be raised for their acorns, which are

Wild Raisin.

used as stock feed or, after some processing, as human food. The American wild persimmon has been developed into several horticultural varieties of great promise.

I have sometimes been tempted to try my hand at this plant-breeding game, and if I ever do, I will work with the genus *Viburnum*. This genus gives us the black haw (V. *prunifolium*), wild raisin (V. *lentago*), American high-bush cranberry (V. *trilobum*), the squashberry (V. *edule*), and several other species with more or less edible fruits. All exhibit very wide seedling variation, and I've found bushes bearing black haws and wild raisins that were certainly good enough to grace any home garden. This fruit would no doubt improve under cultivation.

But what I find exciting about this genus is the large number of only slightly different species, all now bearing edible fruit and blooming more or less at the same time. The possibilities of hybridization are almost infinite—and who knows what strange and delicious fruit might be produced in this manner? If a good fruit is ever produced, there will be no trouble propagating it, for the viburnums submit to grafting, budding, and air-layering, and can even be raised in quantity from rooted cuttings. If any plant breeder starts seriously working with them, I'll bet on his coming up with a new wonder crop in a few years.

Another wild fruit of great promise is the juneberry, also called the shadbush, serviceberry, sarvisberry, sugar pear, and sugar plum. Botanically it is known as *Amelanchier*, and *Gray's Manual* lists nineteen species, most of them so closely related to one another that they can easily form natural hybrids in the wild. At its best, this is already an excellent fruit, and I don't understand why it is not more widely planted than it is. A superb ornamental, its fruit attracts numerous songbirds, and a boy who has never stood by a shadbush and stuffed himself with its delicious fruit just hasn't lived!

This tree's value as an ornamental and a bearer of delicious fruit was appreciated early. The Pilgrim Fathers ate juneberries, and the tree was often planted as an ornamental in Colonial days. George Washington planted sarvis trees at Mount Vernon. It was only later that this fine bush or tree—for no reason that I can discover—became neglected.

Not even the Viburnums offer such possibilities to a dedicated plant breeder as does the sarvisberry. Fortunately, in this case the man for the task has already been found, and he has already progressed far. This is Raymond Nelson, whose Tree Nursery at DuBois, Pennsylvania, specializes in sarvisberries.

Once, on Mount Desert Island of Maine, I was picking some fine sarvisberries that were growing wild by the road. A woman passed by and asked me what kind of berries they were. I gave her all their various names, and then invited her to try them. She ate several handfuls, exclaiming at their delicious flavor, and then said, "Until recently I had no idea how much food could be collected in the wild. Then I read a book called *Stalking the Wild Asparagus*, by Euell Gibbons, which tells about eating all kinds of wild fruits, vegetables, and nuts. You ought to look this book up, for I think you'd enjoy it." I assured her that I would read it at the first opportunity.

Ecology,
Polution,
and
Love

27. What Are Bugs to Do With?

MY little grandson defines everything by function. He is utterly convinced that all nature was created for his own use and enjoyment, so when he meets a new creature or plant, he immediately wants to know how he should relate to it and how it is supposed to relate to him. Once he heard a crow making an awful racket in a nearby tree and asked me what it was. Just then the bird flew up, and I pointed it out to him as the author of all the raucous noise, telling him it was a crow. I could have told anyone what his next question would be. He said, "Grandpa, what is a crow to do with?"

It took a long time to give his question the answer it deserved. As we were riding over country roads, I called his attention to crows eating the bodies of dead animals that had been killed by automobiles and explained that this was a service, for it kept this carrion from becoming foul and dangerous to man. I pointed out crows in winter cornfields and told him how they were eating the larvae of corn borers and how this helped the farmer. I told him the funny story of the Long Island sweet-corn farmers who killed all crows because they were pulling up sprouted corn. Then the farmers had to trap and import more crows—at great expense—because they found that borers were far worse than crows, and they couldn't keep the borers under control without the help of the crows.

I do not share my grandson's beautiful faith that everything in nature is useful, but I do lean in that direction. Had he asked me what a corn borer is "to do with," I would have been hard put to find an answer. It has always been my delight to find use and beauty in those parts of nature that most people consider useless and repulsive. I love crows, bluejays, pigeons, starlings, and sparrows. I like garter snakes, toads, salamanders, and praying mantises. I see beauty in the foliage of the weedy yarrow and in the bloom of the wild carrot. I like bugs and creepy, crawly things, snails and millipedes. I think the iridescent skin of the night crawler is beautiful.

When I was in Hawaii, a friend of mine rented a house to a newcomer to the islands. The next day the newcomer's wife came to my friend almost hysterical. She said the house was infested with lizards. My friend explained that the house was not infested with lizards, but was "furnished" with many geckos, and that these little lizards were a great asset, helping to keep the house free of tropical insects without the use of poisonous sprays that might endanger the health of the new tenants. He talked so convincingly that his new tenant protected the geckos after that and delighted in pointing them out to guests and citing their uses.

One summer up in Minnesota I was fishing from a lake shore with one of my students. Mosquitoes were bothering her, and she turned to me and said, "Mr. Gibbons, what good are mosquitoes?" I had the answer ready for that one. I explained that the larvae of these mosquitoes were an important link in the food chain that made it possible for every fish she was catching to exist in these waters. I then found some pennyroyal, a very fragrant plant of the mint family, and showed her what it was "to do with" by crushing it in my hands and rubbing it on her ankles and face where it served as an organic insect repellent—for mosquitoes don't appreciate that aromatic perfume, although most humans do.

Once in the Southland, I watched a tiny tumblebug laboriously rolling a huge ball of manure many times its own bulk. He rolled it across a little patch of white sand and it became coated with glassy particles. As the sun caught these minute crystals its light was reflected as if from the facets of a finely cut diamond. Suddenly, with a thrill, I knew why the Egyptians had seen in their own dung beetle, the scarab, a symbol of the sun god who brought all life to earth. There was life—in the form of the beetle's egg—in the center of this jewel. The tumblebug labored mightily with his great load, rolled it on and on, until it fell into a crack in the soil. He (or more probably she) didn't attempt to retrieve it, but stood on the edge of the crack and kicked dirt on top of the ball of manure until it was covered, then went about whatever business a tumblebug has.

I sat and reflected on what I had seen. This little bug, by burying that ball of manure, was enriching the soil as well as insuring the propagation of its own species. Billions and billions of such bugs have buried such balls of manure. How much do we owe to such an unnoticed creature—how much of the few vital inches of topsoil on which our own lives depend? Also, by this same effort the tumblebug is ridding the surface of the ground of a dangerous pollution. Has this helped to prevent sickness, and are there people alive today who would be dead if it had not been for the work of the tumblebugs of the world?

My thoughts were half whimsical, half serious. Out came my notebook. In the South, people compose ballads to celebrate great events or to memorialize great tragedies. Why not make a ballad to the scarab?

THE BALLAD OF THE SCARAB

Let's take a trip to Egypt's land
  And sing about a beetle,
Who rolls manure upon the sand
  By Cleopatra's needle.
Despite this lowly job of his
  He's not without some fame,
And *Scarabaeous sacer* is
  His awesome Latin name.

Egyptians did appreciate
  This tumblebug so nimble,
And by a vote of twelve to eight
  Made him the sun god's symbol.
Ten thousand images of him
  In copper, brass, and gold,
And some in stone and precious gem
  Were made by priests of old.

The scarab found a cozy nook
  Within a temple attic,
There saw his picture in a book;
  It made him feel ecstatic.
No wonder he was feeling smug,
  The honor was terrific;
They'd made this humble tumblebug
  Into a hieroglyphic.

"A mere dung beetle," you surmise
  About the scarab small;
You cannot judge him by his size,
  That will not do at all.
You can't dismiss him with a shrug;
  Don't ever try to flout him,

For though he is a tumblebug,
    There's nothing mere about him.

The scarab will ignore your sneers.
    He's proof against your scorn,
He'd been around a million years
    When history was born.
Before the pyramids were raised
    Upon the desert sand
Egyptians sought the scarab's aid
    To sanitize the land.

When Moses led his people out,
    To found the Hebrew nation,
The little scarab was about
    To help with sanitation.
He crept into the private room
    Of Cleopatra fair;
He saw the historic romance bloom;
    Mark Anthony was there.

The scarab heard him threaten her,
    To conquer with his might;
Heard Cleopatra answer, "Sir,
    I am not prone to fight."
He saw the Prophet's horses come,
    Each mounted with an Arab;
It was a time most wearisome
    For patient little scarab.

He had to work both night and day,
    'Twas painful to endure;
It took a week to clear away
    The piles of horse manure.

He later watched a Moslem village
   The day Crusaders came;
He saw them murder, rape, and pillage,
   All in religion's name.

The conquerors have come and gone,
   And each has left his blot,
But still the scarab's rolling on
   The balls of you-know-what.
And so from Cairo to Sudan
   He worked from year to year
As ancient Egypt's only san-
   Itary engineer.

He had to labor all the while,
   Or very soon, methinks,
The smell you'd whiff along the Nile
   Would surely rhyme with Sphinx.
When cause of illness was unknown,
   And knowledge very vague,
The gallant scarab worked alone,
   To save men from the plague.

Had one ancestor caught typhoid
   And childless passed away
Then you'd be nothing but a void—
   You'd not be here today.
So whether you are Greek or Jew,
   Or whether Dutch or Arab,
The chances are you'd not be you
   If there had been no scarab.

Let's give the scarab one big cheer
   And never do him wrong;
It's by his work that we are here
   To sing this silly song.

28. Out in the Garden Eating Worms

IF one always said what one thought, one would have few
friends left. When I hear someone say, "I just love nature,
but I don't know a thing about it," I usually murmur some polite
inanity or say nothing. But I think, "That love of yours must be
either pretty shallow or pretty recent—or you would learn something about nature." Love is a great stimulus to learning, and
nothing else makes study such a pleasure. Besides, how do such
people know that they love nature if they know nothing about
it? It has been my experience that love leads to knowledge and
knowledge leads to deeper and broader love.

Recently a friend who was talking to me as I spaded my
garden gave me an argument on this outlook. She said, "I love
only the beautiful in nature, and it takes no special knowledge to
love brightly colored birds that sing beautiful songs, and pretty
wild flowers that can be made into interesting arrangements.
However," she added, "I simply detest those nasty earthworms
you are turning up." I tried to explain that I would find it difficult to love a robin without loving the earthworm that feeds it

and makes its life possible, and I couldn't love wild flowers without being grateful to the earthworms that made the topsoil in
which they flourish. She persisted, "I can love a beautiful rose
without loving the dunghill from which it grows." Maybe she
can, but I can't. When I look at the rose I see a transformed
dunghill, and when I look at a dunghill I see a mass of potential
roses, and it, too, assumes beauty in my eyes.

How about those "nasty earthworms"? I know these worms
are depositing several tons of castings on my garden every year.
Worm castings are the feces of earthworms—manure—and they
tend to be more neutral than the parent soil, whether this is acid
or alkaline. Worm castings are also much richer in nitrates, organic matter, total and exchangeable calcium, exchangeable
potassium and magnesium, and in available phosphorus than the
soil on which the earthworms fed. I am grateful to the creatures
that work tons of this rich material into my garden soil every
year at no trouble or expense to me, and gratitude is next door
to love.

Depositing castings is only a fraction of the good that earthworms do. They pull organic matter, such as dead leaves, down
under the soil and by their digestive juices break it down into a
form usable by my plants. The environment is enriched by ex-
cretory products other than castings. Their burrows go down as
far as eight feet below the surface, and they bring up rich, un-
touched minerals that my plants need. The burrows improve
aeration, permit the penetration of surface water, and facilitate
the downward growth of roots. Their work improves the tilth, or
workability, of the soil. Every crisp and tasty vegetable I gather
from that garden owes a part of its goodness to those worms,
and I simply cannot think of them as "nasty." Knowledge of
such things is useful to a gardener, but it could be motivated by
greed or gluttony rather than by love. However, as this knowledge grows, you will find yourself loving this lowly creature
despite the possibly selfish nature of the original motivation to
learn something about him. Let's allow this love to lead us to

some not-so-useful but perfectly fascinating facts about this interesting creature. I promise you that learning about earthworms
can be fun.

Some 2,500 species of earthworms have been described by
zoologists, ranging from almost microscopic types to monsters in
South America and Australia that grow to seven feet long and
more than an inch in diameter.

Let's examine a common night crawler, *Lumbricus terrestris*,
and see what we can discover. The family to which this creature
belongs is called *Annelida*, from the Latin word *annelus*, meaning "little ring," and we can readily see that the body is made up
of 100 to 180 ringlike segments, called *somites*, separated by
tiny grooves. Over somites 31 to 37, counting from the head
end, is a conspicuous glandular swelling that is called the *clitellum*, which is the Latin word for pack saddle. The whole body is
covered with a thin, transparent cuticle marked with barely visible cross-striations that produce an iridescence, like mother-of-
pearl, making the worm's body slightly changeable in color as
the light strikes it from different directions. Viewed with an un-
prejudiced eye the earthworm is actually beautiful.

How can the night crawler hold himself so tightly in his burrow? Well, this earthworm has something almost like feet—in
fact he has four pairs of them to each somite, except for the first
three, which are reserved for eating, and the last one, which is
solely concerned with elimination. These almost-feet, called
setae, are small bristle-like chitinous rods. If you look closely,
you can see the lines of paired pores along each side and along
the ventral or bottom part of the worm, through which these
setae can be protruded. Each seta is connected to muscles in the
worm's body and can be moved in any direction, extended or
withdrawn at will. If you try to pull a night crawler from his hole
after he has swelled his body and shoved his setae into the sides
of the burrow, you will merely pull him in two, leaving both you
and the worm looking pretty silly.

How do you tell the males from the females? You don't. Each

night crawler is both a complete male and a complete female. However, this doesn't mean that the worm can go through life and reproduce his kind with no need for contact with others of his species, for the worm cannot fertilize its own eggs. Mating occurs at night in warm, moist weather. Two worms, each leaving the tip of his tail in his own burrow, stretch out and find one another in the dark. The *clitellum*, or pack saddle, on each grips somites 7 to 12 on the other. Special setae on the clitellum of each actually penetrate the body of the other to help hold the worms together, and there is an exchange of masses of sperm. There is thus reciprocal cross-fertilization. This isn't done in a few seconds. The worms secrete a slime covering over themselves and remain in one another's embrace for two to three hours. How come the worm is such a great lover? That one is easy. Each worm has ten hearts, and every sentimentalist knows that the heart is the seat of affection. See! I told you that learning about worms could be fun.

The body of the worm is largely boneless muscle containing rich, complete, and easily digestible protein. Earthworms have been used for food by many primitive tribes. The Maoris of New Zealand consider them a great delicacy. I eat many strange and unusual foods, but even my prejudices start working after a point. I doubt that I could bring myself to eat earthworms until I become hungrier than I have ever been. However, I will not condemn or ostracize those who want to eat this unusual food.

A zoology textbook I own, published about twenty years ago, states: "Ancient medical writers mention various irrational uses of earthworms in human medicine, and they are still followed in parts of Japan and China." Irrational? There is prejudice speaking through supposedly scientific writing if I ever saw it. Modern investigations prove that earthworms have fever-reducing and antiasthmatic properties when taken in medicine, and their bodies are exceedingly rich in provitamin D. I'll bet that "irrational" medicine has more curative powers than many of the drugs for which we pay outrageous prices today.

And now I must confess that there is one way in which worms are not good for a garden, at least not for my garden. I often resolve to spend half a day working in the garden, and this resolve lasts only until I turn up the first spadeful of worm-filled earth. Then I start thinking of the trout stream up the hill, and as soon as I can collect a can of these worms, I'm off fishing. In that compost-fertilized soil the worms get big. A fisherman friend once remarked that I didn't need a hook since the worms from my garden were large enough to choke the fish to death!

I do get back to those weeds in the garden, though. When I return with a string of fish, I go out there and gather some sheep sorrel and purslane to make a wild salad that makes all salads of cultivated greens seem banal and insipid by comparison.

I might also gather some lamb's quarters to cook as a vege-table to go with those fried fish, so fresh from the water that they are almost wriggling when they're dropped into the pan. As I enjoy this sumptuous repast and reflect on how much the earth-worm has contributed to it, I find that despite his contribution to my delinquency, my love for the earthworm has not diminished. Truly, worms are wonderful.

29. The Groundhog
or Woodchuck

THE groundhog is a rodent, closely akin to the rabbit and squirrel, and it is only his piggish eating habbits that have earned him the name "hog." Even his alternate name, woodchuck, means the same thing, for "chuck" is an Old English term for pig. These names were given because of the quantities he eats, and not because of any lack of discrimination, for he is a real epicure, preferring the tenderest and finest organically raised vegetables he can find.

One year a groundhog discovered my organic garden and immediately showed better sense than most humans do by passing up all other foods and living entirely on my very best vegetables. He was very selective, taking the peas only in their sweetest prime, grabbing the green beans when they were at their tender young best, and waiting until the sweet corn had reached absolute perfection before he bothered it. He scorned to eat any vegetable that was still too young to develop its full flavor and refused to touch anything that was even one day too old.

The perfect revenge on such a garden robber would have

been to cook and eat him, thus getting all those vegetables back as meat. An encyclopedia I own said that groundhog meat is "edible but not very palatable." I also remembered a story that was told me by my grandfather about his grandfather. He shot a groundhog with an old cap-and-ball rifle and asked my great-great-grandmother to cook it. She roasted it with sweet potatoes, in the Southern style of preparing opossum, and brought it to the table nicely browned and looking very appetizing. My great-great-grandfather wielded the carving knife with a flourish, then passed the groundhog around the table. His wife, his sons and daughters, his grandchildren, and even the hired man refused to touch it. My ever-so-great grandfather took a piece on his own plate, cut off a bite, and chewed—and chewed—and chewed. Finally he removed the still undivided bite from his mouth and said, "The devil with it; if none of the rest of you will eat it, I'll be derned if I'll sit here and eat groundhog all by myself," and he threw the bite out the open door.

Despite these two unfavorable reports, I still often mentally consigned the groundhog who was pirating my vegetables to the pot. One day when I stepped into my garden he broke from among the green beans and headed for his den, a hundred yards away. This little rodent had been eating approximately as many organic vegetables as my whole family used, and the diet had agreed with him, for it certainly was beginning to show around his waistline. He had become so heavy and ungainly that I could easily outrun him. Quickly I ran between him and his den and then turned to confront him. He came within three feet of me and made a few tentative efforts to pass, but when he saw that I could move faster than he could, he decided to bluff. Pulling back his lips in a phony snarl, he began to snap his big teeth very audibly and started advancing slowly toward me.

I held my ground, and he stopped when only about two feet away. He had apparently played his last card, for the false fierceness slowly drained away. He crouched down and let his fat belly rest on the ground and seemed to be saying that he was prepared to lie there all day until I got out of his way. Avoiding all sudden or quick movements, I lay down in front of him, propping my head on my elbow.

There we lay, eyeball to eyeball, so close together that I could easily have reached out and touched him. I didn't try it, however, for those huge teeth looked exceedingly strong, and I was afraid I might pull my hand back minus a finger. Gradually the look of enmity faded from his eyes. Once he tentatively nibbled a blade of grass, then suddenly, as if he had just realized that he was being impolite, he returned his attention to me. Despite myself, I began to realize that I no longer felt such murderous anger at this garden raider, and then I knew that I could never kill him.

Still, I dreaded expending all that energy raising delicious vegetables for even a charming thief, so I slowly got back on my feet and whistled for a stray dog who had been chiseling handouts around our back door for a few days. The dog came bounding out, came to a stiff-legged halt in front of the groundhog, sniffed a couple of times, then began a cautious advance. But this dog was a once-born soul, loving all living creatures. Next thing I knew, he whined a welcome, began wagging his tail, and started trying to make friends with the groundhog. Disgusted with both the dog and my own chicken-heartedness, I moved aside and let the fat woodchuck escape into his den.

I wish I could report that out of gratitude for my sparing his life the groundhog stopped raiding the garden, but the depredations continued. Finally I could bear it no longer. I built a box trap, baited it with green beans, and set it near his den. The next morning I had him prisoner. I gave him a last good feed of the vegetables he loved so well, then carried him across the mountain to a little uninhabited valley, and released him. He ate a final green bean from my hand, then moved slowly off, dragging his fat belly on the ground.

A few days later my son killed another groundhog while hunting, so I decided to try cooking it, as I felt no affection for this stranger. I was sure my great-great-grandfather had disliked groundhog because he hadn't known enough to remove the glands before cooking it. I carefully removed the four waxy glands, two under the forelegs and two in the small of the back. I carefully cooled the meat for a day, larded it with fat bacon, sprinkled it with tenderizer, and then roasted it with potatoes and onions. When it came to the table, it looked good and smelled good. I took a bite and decided that it was not too unpalatable. I could almost enjoy the flavor. The only trouble was that I was still almost enjoying the same bite ten minutes later without being able to chew it up. Finally I got up and carried the rest of the groundhog outside and offered it to the dog, who was still hanging around. He sniffed at it, then tucked his tail between his legs and trotted off down the road—and I haven't seen him since.

When I told a neighbor about my experiences he explained that it is only half-grown groundhogs that are good to eat. He brought me several of these young ones, and they really are good when cooked by any recipe you would use for a rabbit or squirrel. But I will have to be hungrier than I have ever been before I'll try another old one. Even when eating a young one, the memory of that day when the groundhog and I lay out in that sunny field and gazed into one another's eyes rises in my mind and destroys my appetite for groundhog meat.

From now on, this chubby rodent will be no more than my spring weather prophet, for the groundhog is unique among wild animals in having a special day set aside for it. February 2 is universally known as Groundhog Day. On this date the groundhog is supposed to wake from his long winter's sleep and spend the day aboveground. If the sun is shining and he sees his shadow, he knows that winter is not yet over, so he returns to his den until the Ides of March. But if it is cloudy, and no shadow is visible, then it means an early spring, and the groundhog can stay out. Does this work?

Well, for many years I have noticed that if February 2 is

sunny, then we are due for six more weeks of somewhat warm winter weather, but if that date is cloudy we will have, during the next six weeks, some very cold spring weather. I can understand the groundhog's desire to get an early start on his summer's work, which consists of three jobs: eating . . . and eating . . . and eating.

30. A Moratorium on the War Against Nature

I AM writing this right after a winter storm has broken all records for a December snowfall in this part of Pennsylvania. There would be about two feet of snow on the level—if there were any level—but the wind has made the landscape all ridges and ranges of deep, drifted snow. My study window looks out on an old hillside field that I planted to evergreens a few years ago. Because of fear of injuring or destroying the young trees, I was unable to mow the wild growth in this field, so last fall it was a sea of goldenrod, New England asters, foxtail, and other wild plants, all averaging about four feet high. As I look out now this field is filled with thousands of birds flitting against the snow. Far from suffering a hardship due to the snow, these birds are finding it a new level from which to eat the plentiful weed seeds on the rank dead growth that everywhere comes above the snow.

There is a bird feeder offering some sunflower seeds, mixed bird seed, and suet on our front porch, and it is well attended. But, like me, these birds like to get part of their food from the

Persimmon.

wild. These wild seeds must be special delicacies, for I see some
birds that first stuff their crops at the feeder, then fly out among
the weeds for dessert. Conspicuous against the snow are dozens
of juncos, black-capped chickadees, tufted titmice, and tree
sparrows. The yellow in the scene is furnished by a couple of
hundred evening grosbeaks. Here and there is the bright blue of
a jay, and in a half-dozen places are flashes of red from cardinals. There is even a downy woodpecker, forsaking his trees for
a taste of these weed seeds. I sit here feeling magnanimous because I can furnish this feast for the birds by merely doing nothing but letting nature grow what she wishes to grow. What a
beautiful "crop" of birds I have grown in this old field—and
how nice to have it ripen in all its glowing colors in midwinter,
when all else is dormant or covered with snow!

This same old field has furnished other crops through the
year. About where the red cardinals are foraging was a different
shade of red from Memorial Day until mid-June, when the wild
strawberries ripened—the most bountiful crop in years. In some
spots a man could sit down and pick a quart of these superb
berries without moving. Many quarts of frozen wild berries and
nearly a hundred half-pints of uncooked wild strawberry jam
still stock our freezer, frozen assets for future feasts. Next came

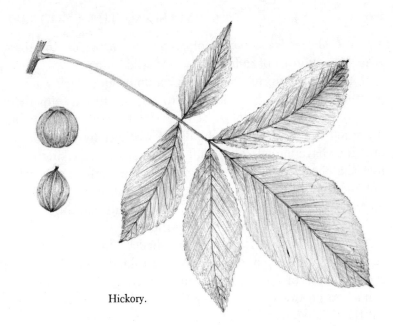

Hickory.

a great abundance of wild black raspberries. These became jam and homemade black raspberry ice cream, so different from the starched, thickened, artificially flavored and colored pastes that sell as ice cream in the supermarkets. Then there were dewberries and high-bush blackberries, all we cared to pick, great in jams, jellies, pies, and fruit soups. Wild cherries were brought in by the pailful for cherry Betty, wild cherry soup, jams, and frozen wild cherries. As summer deepened, elderberries were made into pies, juice, and jelly.

In late fall we gather black haws, not bringing these in but eating as many as we can hold, right from the bush. Some wild fruits should be eaten in the wild.

Along one side of the field, persimmons and hickories grow, yielding the prime ingredients for persimmon–hickory-nut bread, persimmon puddings, and other delicacies. On the other edge, sassafras trees, covered with wild grapevines, lean over the field. We take a few pounds of the sassafras roots for spicy tea and gather enough grapes to make what juice and jelly we can use. We always leave plenty of grapes on the vines, for these attract any number of ruffed grouse and wild turkey.

We race the squirrels for the hickory nuts and black walnuts, but they get their share—not only to eat, but to bury, for these little animals are great forest planters. I often watch them from my study window (when I should be writing) hunting for the nuts they have buried. They sniff and peer about, making tentative scratches here and there, and sometimes actually unearth a nut and then sit up on their haunches to eat it. But a great many must be forgotten, for seedling black walnuts, hickories, oaks, and hazelnuts are coming up all over the field.

Not only nuts and fruits are furnished by this field, but also vegetables. We keep one area heavily manured, and here, before the last frost of spring, we're out gathering winter cress and dandelion greens, well ahead of the first dandelion bloom. We cut the dandelions off well below the ground, remove all outside leaves, and trim away the dark part of the carrotlike root. Then we cut off the tops of most leaves, saving only the very heart of the plant with its tiny, tender leaves and developing bud material. Our freezer holds many packages of these—enough to last until fresh ones are again in their prime. Later in spring we gather fresh poke sprouts, which we peel and blanch, then freeze. Even the rank-growing burdock is welcome in our wild field, for as the stout flower stalks almost leap up, we cut them as low as possible, peel off the bitter outside rind, and slice the centers into white disks to boil until tender—an outstanding vegetable. Bulging at the seams with all these wild goodies, our freezer suggests a "wild party" every time we open the door!

The local Soil Conservationist of the Department of Agriculture sometimes looks askance at the management of this wild field. Recently he came to survey the site of a pond we intend to build in its lower corner. As we walked through the young evergreens, he asked if I intended to get the weed trees out of the field. I explained that what he called "weed trees" I called sugar maples, wild cherries, hickories, black walnuts, persimmons,

31. His Majesty the Monarch

ONE of the most interesting, most beautiful, most conspicuous, and best known of all the butterflies that decorate summer air is the monarch or milkweed butterfly. Originally an American, and still plentiful here, the monarch has also become thoroughly naturalized in Europe, Asia, Australia, and many remote isles of the sea. Its larvae live almost exclusively on plants of the milkweed family, and the present worldwide range of the monarch is mute testimony to the aggressiveness of the milkweed, not a very particular plant, in establishing itself everywhere conditions will permit its growth.

When I first went to Hawaii, the monarch was one familiar note in a largely alien landscape. On inquiry I learned that the butterfly and the milkweed had been introduced together, probably accidentally, about 1850. As tropical sojourners often do, the monarch proved faithless in this romantic setting, deserted the milkweed, and found a new love—the beautiful plumeria, a flowering tree that furnishes the blossoms for some of the loveliest leis with which the Hawaiians express the spirit of aloha.

Monarch pupa.

Monarch.

Monarch larva.

Viceroy.

The plumeria is not a member of the milkweed family; it belongs to the closely allied dogbane family, but it exudes a thick, milky juice that entrances the monarch. Several species of true milkweed now grow in the Islands, and one still sees a few faithful monarchs fluttering near them, but to find large flocks of these red-gold beauties one must find a blooming plumeria.

Although the monarch is extremely widespread and well known, it is far from being a "typical" butterfly, for the species is unique in many ways and has a fascinating natural history. It goes through the usual metamorphosis of egg, larva, pupa, and adult, but it never has an "ugly duckling" stage, being very handsome in all phases. Ordinarily the eggs are laid on milkweed leaves and are tiny, light-green cones of great beauty when viewed under a low-power magnifying glass or hand lens. They hatch, with no attention from the mother, in three to five days, and no one needs to tell the young what to do. They eat day and night, and milkweed is such nourishing food that they reach full size, almost two inches long, in ten to twelve days.

This little caterpillar is one of the gayest creatures alive, zebra-striped in a striking pattern of black, white, and yellow. There is a pair of fierce-looking black horns, or whiplash organs, project-ing over its brow, and a backward projecting pair near the after end of the abdomen, so at first glance it is hard to tell whether the caterpillar is coming or going. When touched, the forward pair of horns twitch nervously, and when the larval monarch walks, these horns have a comical back-and-forth motion that will set you laughing. The larva grows, as all caterpillars do, by shedding its skeleton-skin whenever it becomes too tight, then growing another to fit.

A final shedding and the caterpillar is suddenly transformed into a chrysalis (a bright-colored case in which to pass the pupal stage) that, in my opinion, is the most exquisite jewel produced by the animal kingdom. It is an oblong of beautiful jade green flecked with gold, and even when these golden specks are ex-amined under a lens, it is hard to believe that they are not actu-ally flecks of polished gold leaf, artificially applied. One wonders how a butterfly with a four-inch wingspread can ever fit into this gorgeous green gem. This wonder doesn't cease when, after about twelve days, the chrysalis splits and the large creature crawls forth. Even though the wings are folded and crumpled, it looks absolutely impossible to fit a body so big into a case that small. Moisture flows from the ungainly body into the veins of the wings, streamlining the large abdomen while spreading and stiffening the crumpled wings. In an hour or two, a fully finished monarch, looking new and shiny, waves his wings about a bit to get the feel of things, then takes off as if he had been flying all his life.

Among many moths and butterflies the sexes differ vastly from one another, but the male and female monarch are much alike. In case anyone besides another monarch is interested, the sexes can be told apart. Near the third vein of the hindmost wing, the males have a black spot that is not found on the females. Strangely enough, that extra spot on the males is a little packet of powerful perfume. The male monarch is truly kingly in his attitude toward the opposite sex, and never chases the girls. He just flies leisurely along emitting perfume, and every female that gets a whiff of it comes flying eagerly to him filled with excitement and passion.

Many moths and butterflies live only a few days as adults. Indeed, most such creatures have a far shorter life span as winged beauties than they had as repulsive larvae. Some moths are not equipped to eat at all and can live only until they have used up the flesh bequeathed to them by the fat caterpillars they once were. None of this is true of the monarch. This butterfly has a long, hollow tongue that he usually carries coiled up under his "chin" but which he can straighten to use as a soda-fountain straw to sip sweet nectar from many kinds of flowers. And he has a digestive apparatus that can handle such heady fare. Sustained by these delightful sweets, the monarch lives on and on— as long as ten months—a very long life indeed for a mere butterfly.

This longevity enables the monarch to pull another trick that is rare in the insect world. These butterflies do not hibernate in the winter as eggs, larvae, or pupae the way most of their kind do; they migrate, like birds, and spend the winter in the South. In the fall, great flocks of monarchs gather and head southward. They leave one another plenty of flying room while traveling, but believe in togetherness while resting. Thousands of them will sometimes light on the same tree, suddenly covering it with orange blooms for a few hours. Large flights of monarchs have been reported over outer Cape Cod, showing that these butterflies are not afraid to cross considerable bodies of open water on their long trip from Maine to Florida.

No new generations of monarchs are born in the South. Some of those we see flying south in the fall will survive the winter and return to the milkweed patches of the North in spring. However, even the youngest of them are beginning to feel the effects of old age by the time they reach the new crop of milkweeds, so none of those flying north in the spring will return to the South in the fall. This winter vacation in the sunny South is a once-in-a-lifetime affair for the monarch, so who will blame him if he plays around with a few Florida plumerias while waiting for another generation of milkweeds?

If you think the birds have a feast while the monarchs are migrating, you are wrong. Birds just don't like the taste of monarchs. This brilliant butterfly seems to contradict everything we have learned about protective coloration and natural camouflage, but this is only because we have not learned enough. In studies on the preferences of insect-eating birds, scientists have learned that among over 5,000 species eaten, those *least* preferred were the ones in red, orange, or yellow markings, and among the *most* preferred, *not one species* displayed such colors.

I suspect that the monarch had something to do with the development of this strange taste in birds, for birds find them extremely unpalatable. Even when the bright-colored wings are removed, a caged bird will take only one taste of a monarch and no more. They don't even like the caterpillars. So we see that the brilliant copper-red, orange, and yellow pattern that makes the monarch one of the most conspicuous things in the naturescape is really protective coloration, after all. Those loud colors are like a public-address system constantly repeating, "Don't eat me. I don't taste good."

Another American butterfly takes advantage of the distaste birds show for the monarch. This is the viceroy, a bit smaller than the monarch, but otherwise so closely resembling him in pattern and coloration that birds seem unable to tell the difference between them, so the viceroy shares in the monarch's immunity from attack. The viceroy has a smudgy, curved black line crossing the veins on the hinder wings that the monarch doesn't have—so you can tell them apart, even if the birds can't.

In the viceroy's case, the bright colors are pure deceit, for birds seem to enjoy eating them if the wings with their offending colors are removed.

This is a classic example of mimicry in nature—that is, one creature resembling another in order to gain protection from enemies. The fact that mimicry exists in nature is too well established by evidence to dispute, but it still bothers many students. They want to know how it came about. Surely the viceroy didn't observe that the monarch was free from attacks by birds and decide to resemble him in order to gain the same protection. A butterfly hasn't the reasoning ability to make such a deduction and decision, nor the power to carry it out if it did. I cannot, by taking thought, make one hair of my head black or white, though I know some women who do. Can a viceroy change his spots?

Such impossible assumptions are not necessary to explain how mimicry developed. Let's suppose that the viceroy was once a variable species, and one generation a few of them, by pure coincidence, happened to slightly resemble the monarch. Then the birds would promptly eat those of other colors and patterns, but mistaking these few for monarchs, they would leave them alone, allowing them to survive to become parents of future generations. Obviously, in each succeeding generation those that most closely resembled the monarch would be the ones most likely to survive and bring forth young in their own image. After a few thousand generations of such natural selection by their enemies, the only viceroys left would be those who so closely resembled the monarch that the birds couldn't tell them apart.

You don't have to believe in impossible miracles to discover possible explanations for the wonders of nature, but we do have to believe in the greatest miracle of them all, which is Life— varying, changing, adapting, and surviving. This is Creation, and it is happening now, before our eyes. Is not this wonder enough?

32. The Oldest Living Thing

Nearly every natural-history magazine I pick up these days features an article about "the oldest living thing." It seems that every naturalist in the country wants to present a new candidate for the title, wants to debunk someone else's candidate, or wants to settle the question once and for all.

At the risk of being accused of jumping on the bandwagon when the parade is over, I feel that I simply must get into the act. I want to present some new candidates and to debunk some old ones. But I *don't* want to settle the question once and for all—I want to completely unsettle it, and show why it must remain forever unsettled.

From the time I was a schoolboy right on up until I was pushing middle age the question was considered settled. The General Sherman Tree (*Sequoia gigantea*) in Sequoia National Park in California is still admittedly the *largest* living tree. It is 32 feet in diameter at the base, and measures 18½ feet a hundred feet farther up. It stands 272 feet high, with its largest limb,

130 feet above the base, measuring 6' 2" feet in diameter. There are coast redwoods (*Sequoia sempervirens*) that are taller than the General Sherman by nearly 100 feet, but they don't approach its bulk—an estimated 2,150 tons.

For many years this tree also held the title of the oldest living thing, for it could be proved it was 3,200 years old, certainly an impressive age. Then, in the late 1950s, a naturalist began studying the bristlecone pines of the high mountains of Central California. The size of these trees was not impressive. They usually measure only two to three feet in diameter and less than forty feet in height. However, these trees were obviously ancient. In this arid, high-altitude, inhospitable land they have clung to life for unbelievable lengths of time. At least one bristlecone pine has been proved by ring counts to be an amazing 4,600 years old! This means it was a venerable 1,400 years old before the General Sherman even sprouted from the seed. There is something awe-inspiring about a tree that has been living throughout all recorded history.

Now I'm going to start asking embarrassing questions. Just what do we mean by the oldest living thing? A tree's age and an animal's age are not comparable. To stay alive at all, an animal must remain alive pretty much all over and clear to the center. But a living tree trunk is only alive in a comparatively thin outside layer. Nine-tenths of that massive bulk of the General Sherman Tree is composed of long-dead heartwood. Yet, to stay alive, the tree must continue to grow, for the inside layers of living cells are constantly dying and being added to the dead heartwood. The living foliage is constantly being replaced, even on such evergreens as the giant sequoia. It is very doubtful if any now living part of the General Sherman Tree was alive when I was born, less than sixty years ago.

Still we must admit that the General Sherman has remained an entity, retaining its identity as one tree for all those 3,200 years. Even though the parts of it that were living only a hundred years ago are long since dead, life in this giant tree has been continuous through all these ages.

The case of the bristlecone pine is not quite so clear. This tree attains its great age by periodically sacrificing the greater part of its bulk and concentrating its energy on keeping some of the lower limbs alive. These limbs eventually become secondary trunks, and when they get so large the tree has trouble supporting them, they in turn are sacrificed. Thus it is only the *base* of the bristlecone that has continuously retained its identity as a single tree over those thousands of years. Are those trunks and limbs really all one tree, or are they successively produced vegetative growths from that old base? Some champions of the bristlecone maintain that this is quibbling—that each separate tree grew from a single seed and has had uninterrupted life ever since.

Such a defense would almost certainly rob the bristlecone of its title as the oldest living thing. Once, when I was visiting the mighty coast redwoods, the world's tallest trees, I noticed that some of them seemed to be growing in perfectly straight rows, up to a hundred yards long. My first unthinking notion was that someone must have planted them. But many of these trees are over a thousand years old—and who would have planted rows of redwoods in California a thousand years ago?

Then I came unexpectedly on the answer. A huge redwood trunk lay along the ground where it had been felled by some storm several years before. It had fallen, but it had not really died. All along the trunk, adventitious buds had put out new sprouts that were already on their way to growing up into redwood trees. This mighty mother-trunk could have started in the same way, and the old tree from which it sprang may have started life as still another sprout on another such trunk—and so on back into the dim, prehistoric past.

When one of these redwoods is cut for lumber, the base does not die, but immediately sends up new living sprouts that may grow into marketable trees in sixty or seventy years. Or if not cut, it may survive up to 2,300 years, which is the oldest verified age of a coast redwood. Then, when it finally becomes so top-heavy that it falls in some storm, its life will be continued in dozens of other tree sproutings from its still living trunk. I'm convinced that most of the living coast redwoods have been vegetatively reproduced this way through generations. And almost certainly, some of these magnificent trees owe the life that quickens them to an original seed that sprouted more than 10,000 years ago. See what possibilities this way of computing age opens up? Half of a forest might have descended through vegetative reproduction from that single original seed. Instead of the mightiest tree in the forest being the oldest, that line of hundreds of little sprouts atop the fallen redwood log might, collectively, be the oldest living thing.

The trouble with computing the age of a tree from the time it sprouted from seed—and then counting all subsequent vegetative reproductions as continuations of that same life—is that it opens the door to a vast number of new candidates for the title of "the oldest living thing."

Not far from my home in central Pennsylvania, for instance, grow some colonies of evergreen box huckleberry (*Gaylussacia brachycera*), of a variety that produces infertile seeds. Obviously, all these colonies started from a single seed growing into a single plant and multiplying by sprouts from underground rhizomes. Judging from the distance these colonies have traveled from one another, and checking this with certain geological clues, scientists estimate these colonies to have been continuously alive for 13,000 years! That makes the bristlecone pine look like a youngster.

Don't come running up to Perry County, Pennsylvania, though, to gaze on the oldest living thing. There is something singularly unsatisfying about several colonies of plants being given this distinction. No one even tries to maintain that the original bush is still standing. There is nothing of great antiquity to be seen.

If we admit this colony of huckleberries for the title, then we have completely lost the certainty of ever pinning the honor on anything. It is only because of a fluke mutation in which a seedling berry bush lost the ability to bear viable seeds that we are able to estimate the age of this particular colony of box huckleberries.

This doesn't mean that many other colonies of plants with the ability to put up new sprouts from rhizomes may not be even older than these evergreen huckleberries. Those little wintergreen or teaberry plants have thin stems that run just below ground and put up tiny plants bearing bright-red berries with a sprightly wintergreen flavor. I have traced some of these underground stems for many yards, past many forkings. Often what appears to be an extensive patch is only a large number of aboveground branchlets from one extensive underground stem. If these stems are broken, the plant does not die, but merely takes up existence as two independent plants. Sections of the colonial plant can be destroyed without wiping out the life that originally came from one seed. Even while gazing on the box huckleberries of unauthenticated age, I wondered if the little wintergreen plants growing under them might not be older. There is simply no way we can know.

The honor may even belong to some humble, non-woody, herbaceous plant such as the milkweed or dogbane. These put up, aboveground, fruiting and seeding plants that last only one season—but life goes on in the underground rhizomes that push on, fork, and sprout new plants endlessly and with apparent immortality. When we merely look at the aboveground parts of one of these plants, we simply don't know whether it is this year's seedling or whether it springs up from a rhizome that could be the bearer of life that came from a seed 15,000 years ago.

If we want to get back to a single, observable, identifiable oldest plant, then I have still another candidate to offer as a potential rival for the giant sequoia or the basal parts of the bristlecone pine. This is the primitive, lowly little lichen that grows on vertical rock faces in the Arctic and Antarctic. These plants are formed by a strange partnership between certain algae and fungi. Several kinds of lichen grow on bare, vertical rock surfaces where they face no competition from other forms of plant life. They produce an acid that dissolves the tiny amount of minerals they need out of the solid rock. Furnished water by rains and fogs, they manage to synthesize a little food from air, light, and water in the few chlorophyll-containing cells found in their leaflike growth called the *thallus*. The lichen is a living plant, but most of the time it doesn't do anything. It just sits there, stays alive, and grows older.

It is already known that some lichens are very old. Two photographs of the same plant, taken ten years apart, may show no discernible difference. Growth is infinitesimally slow, and yet some of these lichens grow larger than your hand. Occasionally, pieces of the thallus fall off, or may be knocked off by hailstones or accidents. But this no more ends the life of lichens than the fall of autumn leaves terminates the life of deciduous trees. If some dedicated scholar determines the growth rate of lichens, or the rate at which the rocks are worn away by lichen acid, or any method by which we can determine the age of individual lichens, I would not be surprised to learn that some of these tiny, insignificant plants are as much as 30,000 years old—or more!

I hope that I have so thoroughly unsettled this question that every reader will now realize the futility of searching for the oldest living thing. The big trees of California and the ancient bristlecone pine forests are well worth seeing, but let us not burden them with superlatives they cannot honestly claim. If you yearn to see a miracle of long, continuing life, just open your eyes and look about you. Did you ever split open a seed and examine the tiny embryonic plant within it, complete with beginning stem and two tiny leaves? Was not this life once part of the life of the parent plants, and does not their life continue when the seed sprouts and grows?

The case is even plainer with higher animals. A living haploid cell from the father's body combines with a living haploid cell from the mother's to form a new living diploid cell that divides and redivides until the offspring is a miniature likeness of its parents before it is expelled from its mother's body. Does not the parents' life continue in this young one?

Why rush about seeking miracles of longevity when we are surrounded with miracles of immortality? Are not the mighty sequoias awe-inspiring enough without being revered because they are a mere 3,000 years old? If the persistence of life through long ages thrills you, just gaze on the nearest living thing, and realize that the life in it has probably been continuous since the first living cell appeared on this planet—about *two billion* years ago! I have thrilled to this miracle for over fifty years, and the contemplation of it fills me with a deep love and respect for nature, and an even deeper love and reverence for the Author of nature, the Creator of the miracle called Life.

33. Wild Prejudice

I ONCE heard a so-called survival expert say that wild-plant foods were useless in survival situations because it took more energy to digest wild plants than they could furnish. I sat there wondering how millions of primitive peoples throughout the world—who eat nothing but wild-plant foods for long periods of time—stay alive. The truth is that such statements are the worst kind of nonsense, and the fats, proteins, and carbohydrates of wild-plant foods are just as easily digested and just as nutritious as those from domesticated plants. It pays to keep a wary eye out for the pseudo-scientist who is trying to present logical and reasonable excuses for his illogical and unreasonable prejudices.

While I was doing some beachcombing à la carte in Hawaii, a doctor friend expressed disgust at my largely wild-food diet. When I challenged him to justify his attitude he said, "I suppose it is because my profession makes me so conscious of sanitation." He probably hadn't thought before speaking, for he was not a stupid man—but he had given a very stupid answer. The tropical fruit in which I reveled had been gathered from deep in the jungles and high in the mountains, far from the haunts of men. It had never been touched by human hands until I came to claim it. In contrast, the produce of the stores had been handled by farmers, laborers, and customers, some with dirty hands, perhaps even some with diseases. It had been raised in air that may have been polluted, irrigated with polluted water, and sprayed and fertilized by chemicals. My own wild food was clean because it had never had an opportunity to become dirty.

An irate "expert" wrote to a publication in which my book *Stalking the Wild Asparagus* was reviewed, saying that such an "ignorant food faddist" should not be allowed to publish such books. He was upset because I had recommended pigweed or lamb's quarters, which he said contained poisonous oxalic acid, as a cooked vegetable. I wrote him a polite letter pointing out that spinach, chard, and beets all contained as much oxalic acid as lamb's quarters, or more. I also mentioned that lamb's quarters had been eaten by millions of country people for centuries with apparent benefit, and that it commonly appeared in the vegetable markets of a number of countries. I asked him if he felt the same kind of animosity toward people who recommended the domestic vegetables that contain traces of oxalic acid, which is apparently wholesome in small quantities. He didn't write back.

Now why do you suppose this man was so upset at the suggestion that one could eat a common wild plant? Obviously it wasn't really because the plant contained minute quantities of oxalic acid, or else his ire would have extended to other sources of the material. Somehow, many feel menaced by undomesticated nature, and I suspect his pique was more because the plant was wild than because he thought it poisonous.

A few years ago, near Philadelphia, a child died from eating the berries of horse nettle (*Solanum carolinense*). Unfortunately, a reporter was careless about identification, and wrote that the plant was a ground cherry. The next day the paper printed a retraction, but the damage had been done. A child dying of eating a wild plant is dramatic, and the story was

Ground Cherry.

picked up by the press all over the country. But a retraction is a dry, un-newsworthy bit, so they ignored it. Since I had recommended the ground cherry in one of my books, I became the target for a barrage of letters and phone calls.

A mother called and asked how she could completely eradicate the ground cherry in her neighborhood. I told her the guilty plant was not a ground cherry—which, I added, is a perfectly wholesome and delicious fruit even though it is distantly related to the fatal plant. She replied that she would like to eradicate all relatives of that vicious plant. I told her this might get her in trouble, as potatoes, tomatoes, eggplant, and green peppers are all as closely related to the horse nettle as is the ground cherry. As far as I can discover, this is the first and only death ever reported caused by this plant. The horse nettle berry tastes so nauseating that it would be extremely difficult for a person with a normal sense of taste to eat enough for it to be fatal. And yet the panic displayed was unbelievable. Frightened parents demanded that all waste areas be sprayed with herbicides to kill off all wild growth, or that hundreds of men be hired to burn off all wild areas with flame-throwers. Others demanded that all open places be paved.

Meanwhile hundreds, even thousands, of children were dying from being poisoned by aspirin, sleeping pills, and tranquilizers they took from the medicine cabinets in their own homes—and no one was getting excited about it. Man has become so alienated from nature that he doesn't consider it nearly so horrible to die of some civilized, processed product of our technology as he does from some intrusion of the small area of nature that still is not under man's control.

A boy in Ohio became ill, and from his symptoms it was suspected that he had been bitten by a brown recluse spider. On this slim evidence the public panicked. Demands poured in that the state government do something about this horrible menace. And the things they wanted done were chemical. They wanted the whole state so soaked in poison that no brown recluse could survive. Actually it is a small, rather inoffensive, spider that is very rare, only four specimens ever having been collected in Ohio. Sometimes it hides in lumber piles in dark cellars and, while its bite is dangerous, it doesn't attack, but merely bites when inadvertently pressed or squeezed, stepped on, or otherwise threatened. If one actually tried to exterminate this spider by aerial spraying, there would be little else alive when the last hidden recluse died.

Millions of people pass through Yosemite Park every year, and a few years ago, for the first time, some bears attacked campers. This was probably the campers' own fault—although the attack has never been adequately explained—but again there was public panic. A woman wrote that her family had planned a camping trip that included Yosemite Park, but they were calling it off unless I could tell them how to protect themselves from bears. I wrote back, explaining that one did not keep candy bars or tempting foods in the tent when bears were about, that one did not provoke the bears, did not feed them, and did not try to pet them. Then I pointed out that, statistically, her family was about a million times more apt to die in a traffic accident between Pennsylvania and California than they were to be even slightly molested by the bears after their arrival, and I wondered why this hazard didn't seem to worry her. It seems that we find civilized hazards—such as traffic, sprays, and other processed poisons—perfectly respectable, but the wild ones are thoroughly disreputable.

Do you wonder why we cannot rally public support to vitally needed conservation measures? As long as people consider nature in the wild a menace to be avoided and eliminated, we won't get support for measures to preserve it. And our future lives depend on getting conservation measures started as soon as possible. The time is already late. At the present rate that air pollution is increasing, some cities could become uninhabitable before 1980. Cities are crying for water. The country is gradually being hidden under our discarded waste. Even well water is becoming undrinkable in many cases because of chemicals we use on soil and in our technology. Many species of wildlife are threatened with extinction—and every time man exterminates another species through his carelessness or greed, all mankind is diminished. Our pollution has moved out over the world, and DDT is found in the fat of penguins in Antarctica.

How are we to turn this tendency around before it is too late? I maintain that no effective conservation program can be implemented until this fearful public attitude is changed. How are we to change it?

We must not try to pretend there are no hazards in nature in the wild, but we can easily demonstrate that most of our risks disappear when one is armed with knowledge. Even at their worst, the hazards of nature are not nearly as dangerous as those of this overcivilized world—and very far from being as dangerous as those unacquainted with nature believe them to be.

There is no short cut. A changed attitude will come about only with an increase of knowledge about nature, and this can be gained only through greater intimacy with nature and having creative encounters with her. Only when we have discovered that Mother Nature can truly be a mother will we learn not to hate, fear, and fight her, but to love, cherish, and protect her. Are you passing on wrong—and ultimately destructive—attitudes to your child?

Next week I am taking two boys on a week-long camping trip. We will take only flour, raw sugar, salt, and cooking oil. All the rest of our food will come from fish, frogs, turtles, crayfish, and other aquatic life we catch, and from the wild fruits and vegetables we can find and gather.

I have tried this before, and each such trip turns into a continuous feast. We will breakfast on elderberry flower fritters, and thick black-raspberry flummery. We'll lunch on wild salads, blueberry dumplings, and wild cherry tarts. There will be fish baked with wild onions and sheep sorrel, salads of watercress, purslane, cattail hearts that taste like cucumber, and bright-red wintergreen berries to add a jolly taste, some calamus to provide a gingery flavor, and some mulberries just for fun.

The boys are wildly excited about the trip, and I know from previous experience that they will not be disappointed. And I also know that after this trip they will not think of nature as an enemy to be conquered, but as a friend to be saved from man's brutality, thoughtlessness, and greed. They will have become conservationists.

34. Where Did We Go Wrong?

AMERICA is in a mess that is rapidly growing worse. Everyone knows that we can't continue down the road we have been traveling without meeting major disasters. Already we have met disasters that are not minor. Our cities cry about water shortage while wading knee-deep in sewage. Great rivers and lakes have become so polluted that they will no longer support life, and their waters have become unusable. Every year we cover more of our fertile earth with strips of concrete, and use more land to serve as graveyards for our worn-out automobiles.

Sometimes we think we see hope that this disastrous trend is being reversed. There was our former First Lady's beautification program, the clean stream law, air-pollution legislation, clean-up campaigns and a growing interest in conservation. My advice is not to put too much trust in these palliative measures. They are mainly attempts to alleviate the results—rather than to remedy the cause—of our national ills. They are slaps at the symptoms rather than a cure for the disease. The primary pollution, out of which all other pollution flows, is the pollution of our ideas, our philosophy, and our attitudes.

Did you ever consider how "respectable" the sources of some of our worst pollution are? I'm afraid we often tend to think of pollution in terms of the trash unthinkable vandals dump along our streams. Litter is an unholy and unsightly mess, but the real damage it does cannot be compared to that done by the waste flowing from perfectly respectable paper mills, or being flushed from beautiful yachts. These wastes are the kinds that cause a vast proliferation of microscopic life that uses up all the available oxygen in the water, suffocating all higher forms of life and making a river or lake into a dead, stinking sewer.

In the same fashion, the pollution of our attitudes and philosophy comes from eminently respectable sources. Those great naturalists, Darwin and Wallace, shared a fallacy that has since been discredited. They thought that environment brought about certain acquired changes in characteristics of a species, and that acquired characteristics could be passed on to the progeny. If such changes had "survival value" they were likely to be preserved in the species by "natural selection" and cause the rise of new and different species. Since their time, numerous experiments have satisfied all reputable scientists that acquired characteristics cannot be inherited, but this theory, based on false presumptions, hit society at an unfortunate time and is still coloring our thinking about nature. Competitiveness, aggressiveness, and dominance were at that time being hailed as the most desirable characteristics that anyone could possess. Darwin and Wallace did not say that these were the characteristics most likely to survive, but many of their followers implied that the fittest meant the creature that was most domineering, violent, and combative.

The great genius Thomas Huxley, while one of the first to challenge this theory of "gradualism" in evolution, loved to emphasize the violent competitiveness and overpowering aggression in nature. The great Victorian poet Tennyson used such phrases as "Nature, red in tooth and claw," and our own William James, while deploring the growing softness of our young people, urged that they be enlisted in "man's eternal war on nature."

Despite scientific refutation, this fallacy has persisted into our day, and is still found in the most respectable quarters. One of the greatest minds of our time, Arnold Toynbee, in his book *An Historian's Approach to Religion*, speaks of "Nature's lust and bloodthirstiness," and even writes—and I quote, "The first aspect in which Nature presents herself to Man's intellect and will is as a monster who is creating and destroying perpetually, prodigally, aimlessly, senselessly, ruthlessly and immorally."

I pity a man who can see nature only through such eyes. When I hear a man using such phrases as "Nature's lust and bloodthirstiness" and "Nature, red in tooth and claw," I think that here is a man who is getting his attitude toward nature from books, and not from firsthand observation. If man is really engaged in "eternal war on nature," then I am a traitor to mankind, for I have withdrawn from this war and made a separate peace.

In the same book I have mentioned, Dr. Toynbee says, "Every living creature is striving to make itself the center of the universe, and in the act is entering into rivalry with every other living creature." A good course in ecology would have kept this truly great man from making such a ridiculous statement. It ignores the vast community of cooperation, interdependence, symbiosis, commensalism, and mutualism that is found within nature. It would be far more true to say that every life form, in order to survive, must relate itself to dozens of other life forms, and the vast majority of these interrelationships could never be described as rivalry. I do not ignore the competition and violence that is found in nature. Of course these things exist. But when viewed in the context of the interdependence and the great areas of cooperation found in nature, the roles of competition and violence are seen to be pretty small.

The concept of the "survival of the fittest" certainly has some validity, but it is a great error to suppose the fittest to be the most violently competitive. The science of paleontology has made findings that seem to indicate that the most rapacious creatures tend to die out, become extinct. The meek often do inherit the earth. The fittest, the creature that survives, is apt to be the species that has best learned to cooperate with other life forms around it.

We sometimes see this cooperation in nature become so important that two separate species become absolutely dependent on one another for survival, and this is what we call a symbiotic relationship. The common termite cannot exist except in partnership with a protozoan that changes cellulose into a form which can be digested by the insect, and the protozoan cannot exist without the termite to masticate the wood cells on which it lives. A great many plants cannot produce seeds without certain insects to pollenize their flowers, and these insects cannot exist without exactly these plants on which to feed.

In other cases the cooperation is not so absolute, and then it is called mutualism—two species helping to fill one another's lives and make them worth living. This kind of cooperation exists all around us if we only open our eyes to see it. I find nature overflowing with unexpected kindnesses and mercies. Near my home there is a wild persimmon tree that produces some of the most delicious fruit I ever tasted. Why do you suppose this tree has seen fit to surround its seeds with these sugary lumps of goodness? It is so it can offer this tempting food as a free gift to passing animals—so they, in turn, will help to scatter its seeds, thus helping to disseminate and propagate the species. It grows those fine fruits so I'll pick them and eat them. I could exist without this persimmon tree, and it could exist without me, but both our lives are richer because we have a relationship.

35. Pollution and Love

D ON'T drink the water, don't breathe the air. And keep
your eyes tightly closed so you can't see how ugly our
beautiful country is becoming. America seems to have finally
opened those eyes. Last year, hundreds of thousands of students,
ecologists, conservationists, naturalists, sportsmen, and just
plain concerned citizens held a series of meetings, rallies, and
days of concern, or Earth Days, to see what could be done about
our rapidly deteriorating environment due to pollution, littering,
and overpopulation. Since these rallies were spread over several
days I managed to lecture at three of them, one in Connecticut,
one in Philadelphia, and one in Pittsburgh. I was asked to lecture at several more gatherings, but couldn't make them all. I
am very pleased at this evidence that some people believe my
non-violent approach to nature has value, and that some realize
that my interest in nature extends beyond the gourmet foods she
can furnish me.

At these gatherings I met hundreds of young people, most
with long hair, the men with beards. They were dressed in the
very height of fashion—that is, their sneakers exactly matched
their sweatshirts. I found these young people serious and truly

concerned about the erosion of the quality of life due to the massive befouling of the earth, air, and water. They are willing and eager to bring youthful energy, dedication, and intelligence to the conservation cause, and this is the most hopeful sign that I have seen that the present destructive trend might be reversed. I was so impressed by these young idealists that I determined I would never again be put off by hair.

As a symbol of my solidarity with these shaggy young conservationists, I have declared my own head a natural area. Whether it is because some of the wild herbs I eat have hair-growing properties, or because I happened to select the right ancestors, as I push sixty years old I still have a very heavy head of hair. I must admit that I am finding this long hair a nuisance, too hot and too hard to care for, so as soon as I have convinced some of the youngsters that they have no monopoly on either concern for the environment or the ability to grow hair, I think I'll shorten it.

Many of these youngsters are angry, and I can't blame them. We are passing on to them a far dirtier environment than the one we received when we were their age.

I find the anger justified, but I hope today's youth will act out of their genuine concern for a better world, and not out of their anger. Too many of them saw the situation as a battle between them and the establishment. I believe that concern and dissent should be expressed, but I want to see some of those brilliant young minds go to work on means of expressing it in love, not hatred. I oppose name-calling, violence, and even some forms of militant pressure, not only because they are wrong, but because they are stupid. Inevitably, such tactics delay solution of the problem. Battle lines that are drawn must be undrawn before anything can really be done. Let us admit right now that even the polluting industrialist is a human being, who loves and is loved. Let our own humanity and love speak to his humanity and love in working for a better environment. Ultimately, all quarrels must be settled by communication, negotiation, goodwill, and mutual respect for one another's humanity, regardless of how much fighting has gone before.

Let's take a shortcut. Strike violently at an industrial polluter and he will strike back, defending even his wrongdoing. Zap him with love, and he is left helpless to do anything except repent and change. As Paul said, "Thus may you heap coals of fire on the tops of their heads." I saw many buttons on sweatshirts reading "MAKE LOVE NOT WAR," so let's apply that slogan to the home front. Apply those well-trained minds and that boundless energy to finding creative ways to use love in the struggle for a saner environment. Eventually, our conservation and ecological problems must be solved that way; why not now?

In one city where I lectured, the young people went out along the highways and through the parks and picked up all the nonreturnable beer and soft drink bottles, and all aluminum beverage cans. These were sorted according to brand, and all breweries and bottling companies who had local offices found these unsightly objects dumped on their lawns and office entrances. This was a very clever and dramatic way to draw these companies' attention to the part their product was playing in the accumulation of unsightly litter, but did it really do anything to solve the problem? Most beverage companies can point out that they still offer their product in returnable bottles, and that the beer or soft drinks are actually offered at a lower price in these return-deposit bottles, but that the public is demanding the convenience of no-deposit, non-returnable containers. They can also show that in this affluent society almost as many returnable bottles become litter as do the non-returnables. How can we apply love to this situation in a way that offers some possibility of solving the problem?

It might require more dedication and sacrifice than these youngsters are willing to give, but I doubt it. Suppose a group of these serious young people pledge enough time and work to keep an area completely clean of litter. They could still count brand names and inform the guilty companies regularly about the quantity of their particular litter that was being picked up, and how long it takes to do it. They could even claim that they had voluntarily entered a form of slavery which would continue until the company changed its method of merchandising. They could beg the company to emancipate them. They could also urge boycotting such products. This would offer a creative and economically feasible alternative to the present unacceptable policy which even the beverage companies know cannot be continued indefinitely, or we will be walking the earth on a ten-foot-deep junkpile made up of cans and non-returnable bottles.

I am no genius, but I doubt that it takes one to think up a simple and economical answer to this problem. We might propose that all bottlers agree to use identical, returnable bottles. Labels and caps could vary to individualize each company's product. We could further propose a requirement for a deposit of 10¢ per bottle, either by mutual agreement or by legislation. This would not increase the cost of the beverage—indeed, it might materially lower it.

It would not cost the consumer more except for the first purchase, and he would be repaid quickly with the containers he returns. Empties would be universally returnable for the deposit. Then, if some heavy-pocketed slob threw a bottle by the roadside, some kid or some wino seeking enough for another drink would pick it up and return it. These bottles would be as good as sterling in any store.

I can't imagine the news media or the public being hostile or even unsympathetic to such action and such proposals. The first company to use the high deposit would be sure to get unlimited national publicity, gaining sympathy and causing new adherents to come pouring in. I believe that other companies would shortly capitulate. If a company dragged its feet, we might try a new picketing tactic. The prettiest girls to join the movement (they all look beautiful to me) would be set to making Hawaiian flower leis. They would appear at the companies' head offices just at quitting time. As each executive walked out, he would be necklaced with flowers accompanied by the traditional kiss. Only then would the girl ask him what he was doing to change the company's destructive policy. It's bound to work. There is no defense prepared against love.

In another city where I lectured during the conservation furor, young conservationists publicly displayed the brand names of the various household detergents and indicated how much phosphate each one contained. There were a number of tables presided over by attendants who would wrap and mail back to the company any partly used box of the detergent that anyone would bring in with a letter explaining that the sender would not buy any more of this product until the water-polluting phosphates were removed. Most of the sewage in this country, after more or less treatment, eventually empties into streams. Phosphate pollutes because it is a good fertilizer, causing a vast proliferation of microscopic life in the stream. These organisms demand so much oxygen that all dissolved oxygen is used up, and then the fish and other freshwater life forms die of drowning. Yes, a fish can drown if the water he breathes contains insufficient oxygen.

This "Operation Mailback" probably comes under the heading of permissible pressure. I'll bet that at least some of the companies affected set aside more money for research on nonpolluting detergents. (One already exists, and we use it, but I'm afraid some of the youngsters would consider it a new invention. It is called laundry soap.) The main objection I have to this attention-getting pressure method is that it won't begin to do the job that needs doing.

Do you think it would be all right to release the effluent from the sewage treatment plant into the stream, provided the phosphates were removed from the detergents? Not on your life! Human beings produce a product that is rich in plant nutrients, and it, too, can cause proliferation of oxygen-consuming organisms. We can't very well demand that this be cleaned of all pollutants at the source. The products of garbage disposal units are also very rich pollutants of the same kind. Even the dirt we wash from our clothes, dishes, and bodies can cause a rise in oxygen demand.

A sewage-treatment plant can remove the solids from this fertile sewage, kill some of the dangerous disease germs, and clarify the water, but it can't remove those dissolved mineral plant foods that cause the main trouble. If you eliminated the phosphates contributed by detergents, how much cleaner would the stream be? I want a solution that solves the whole problem, and preferably one that solves several problems at once.

Here the solution is obvious to any organic gardener. It is excellent plant food that is polluting the stream. Why turn the rich effluent into the stream at all? Let's run it the other way, put it on plants, and let them use this fertilizer to promote their own growth. They can use the water, too. The plants will remove the pollutants and use the water. Much of it will be expired by these plants to God's great distillery and fall again as pure, life-giving rain. The part that seeps away through the ground will be filtered through miles of earth and finally enter the stream as crystal-clear, cold, pure water. Besides polluting the stream, we are, under present methods, wasting a very valuable resource in that dissolved plant food.

Do you think it degrading to eat food plants raised in your own sewage? You do it every day. How about the market gardener downstream who is using polluted water for irrigation? Would you feel the same way about using your own sewage to grow feed crops, such as field corn, hay, and ensilage crops, which we eat only after they have been transformed by animals into meat, milk, and eggs? After all, we eat foods all the time that were fertilized by untreated animal manure. Maybe we should play fair and let the animals have feed treated by our wastes. That way we could shuttle these valuable minerals and organic materials back and forth between us without ever wasting them. This would bring us into a community of cooperation with our domestic plants and animals, a symbiotic relationship, and that is what ecology is all about.

Even if the public proved so squeamish that they would not

accept the use of this sewage as agricultural fertilizer, there is another inspired use for it, and this is the solution that I would like to see, because it solves more than one problem. All over the country you see scars on the land made by men—vast areas where strip mining, extraction of earth for building fill, gravel pits, and other man-made erosion have disfigured the landscape. If we sent this liquid sewage to these areas in huge pipe lines and sprinkled about two inches a week on these sterile areas, they would immediately begin to grow real forest trees. Under such ideal conditions they would grow very rapidly. In most cases state or federal government could acquire these blighted, mined-out areas for a song, and in a few years they would be marvel-ously green parks with all the man-made scars hidden.

This method is already in use in southern Ohio, and the same pipeline that carries the life-giving sewage to the worked-out strip mines is used, by reversing the flow, to carry granulated coal, in water, back to the cities to run their power plants and industry; this has proved to be the cleanest and by far the best way to transport coal.

We might even do better than that. Most sewage-treatment plants are no more than huge septic tanks, using microorganisms to break down the sewage and liquefy most of it. In this organic process, huge quantities of methane, or marsh gas, are produced. This is an odorless, colorless, highly inflammable and commer-cially valuable gas. It could be used to run municipal power plants and would give off far less pollution than does coal, or even oil. It could be liquefied for country homes, or it could be used to run cars and trucks with some decrease in the amount of pollution petroleum-burning vehicles shoot into our already overburdened air. Or it could merely be added to the municipal gas supply.

I would also like to suggest that the rights of way for these pipelines be improved for bicycle paths. Millions of Americans, young and old, would like to take a cycling trip but won't risk life and limb on our crowded, speed-mad highways. Every vacationer who can be removed from a car and put on a bicycle will reduce the air pollution from automobile exhausts by just that much.

Now, let's look back at those phosphates we discussed. If the above method were followed, we could get off the detergent maker's back. The more phosphates he put in his products, the better, for it would help the trees to grow. By making our sewage-treatment plants of large enough capacity we could not only encourage the use of garbage disposal units, we could require them, just as we now require flush toilets in urban habitations. Even the organic gardeners could rest comfortably in the knowledge that their garbage was being used in a good cause. This would eliminate garbage collection, another big saving.

Wouldn't this all be prohibitively expensive? I honestly believe it would prove to be a good investment, rather than an expense. But how can parks and woods be made to yield a cash return? Don't you know that outdoor recreation areas are the modern gold mines? If nothing else was done to the blighted strip-mine areas besides making them grow up in trees and blossom like a rose, they would still be very valuable. With all that production of browse, they could support huge game populations of deer, bear, turkey, and grouse. Back in the Fifties, the state of Utah computed that out-of-state hunters coming there for mule deer paid an average of $7 per pound for all the deer killed. The same year, Oregon found it was getting about $10 per pound for the trout caught by visitors. This included all the hunter paid for transportation, food, lodging, liquor, equipment, licenses, and the hire of local guides. These luxuries have not declined in price—in fact, I'll bet both states are getting twice as much for their game and fish today. The cost above the price of butcher's meat represents what the sportsman is willing to pay for the recreation of a hunting or fishing trip. He doesn't feel at all cheated, which is more than I can say after a trip to the butcher shop. Now you see what these new wild and beautiful areas could mean to the state?

36. Let's Get Everybody into the Act

WE'VE already discussed ways of eliminating can and bottle litter and how to stop the pollution of streams by detergents and sewage. How about industrial wastes as stream polluters? We need a new concept of private property, capitalism, and the competitive, free-enterprise system. Who owns the air? Who owns the streams? Who owns the natural beauty of an area? You and I do. Every citizen of this country, be he property owner or pauper, has a sizable fortune tied up in such real, but frozen, assets.

Industrial plants as they are operated today cannot confine the pollution they produce to their own property. A company whose smokestack pollutes your air, causing you sickness or discomfort, or merely depriving you of a transparent medium through which to look at natural beauty, is infringing on your property rights and should be held responsible. A supersonic jet that puts those plaster-cracking, window-breaking, nerve-shattering sonic booms into your air is infringing on your property rights in several ways, and the cost of compensating you should be figured into the price of operation, which would probably make economic nonsense of the whole endeavor.

When the waste products of an industrial plant are turned into a stream, forcing all downstream cities to install expensive water-purification plants, then every person whose water rates are consequently raised is subsidizing that plant's product. And this is not proper capitalism. These companies may point proudly to the new jobs they are creating, and the handsome profits they are returning to stockholders, but if they are able to do this *only because they are not paying the full cost of producing their product*, then we should audit our books carefully and see if possibly they are more of a liability than an asset.

When any industrial plant discharges pollution into the air or water and we are within range of its filth, then the product it is manufacturing is being subsidized by you, me, and thousands like us, who neither work for the company nor hold stock in it, and probably do not even use its product. *The cost of any product must include the cost of disposal of the waste products incidental to its manufacture that does not harm anyone else in any way.* Let's throw the concept of the "rights of private property" back into the faces of those who so valiantly defend it, the industrial managers, and demand that they either cease infringing on our property rights or else compensate us adequately for doing so. If the courts decide that they must pay for the very real damage they are doing to those who suffer through their pollution, then we'll see those wastes disappear from our air and water in double-quick time.

Sometimes, the violation of our property rights is indirect. I live several miles from the Susquehanna River, but its proximity is one of the reasons I moved here. It is still far from being a clean stream, but it is getting better every year as the anti-pollution laws are being enforced, albeit with great reluctance and dragging of feet. I use this river for fishing and canoeing. This recreation is worth real money to me, and I paid real money to get where it could be enjoyed. Now, suppose a vegetable and fruit cannery is installed upstream, and they turn all their wastes into the river, creating such oxygen demand that the fish all die. The fishing would be at an end, and I can't enjoy canoeing in a stream filled with visible, and smellable, cannery wastes and dead fish. To get the recreation I need for a balanced life I would then have to pay out considerable sums for transportation, lodging, and other expenses of traveling to a stream clean enough for my purposes. The ready accessibility of the Susquehanna gives my place part of its value, value that is lost if the river becomes unusable. Should I not be compensated for these losses, which were directly caused by the company and are in no way my own fault?

"But where can we dispose of these wastes?" the industrialists cry.

The answer is that our throw-away culture must come to a screeching halt. All that is presently called "waste" must be considered potential raw material to make other products we can use. An army of researchers must be set to work to find profitable uses for what we now throw away. "Profitable" in this case means any use that disposes of these polluting materials less expensively than our present polluting practice of throwing them away, and in all the costs we must figure in the damage to humans and to the environment and the general lowering of the quality of life, if one can put a price on such precious things. Let's look at some of the clever work that has already been done in this field.

As far back as 1947, a microbiologist named Harry Humfeld had discovered ways of growing mushroom mycelium in cannery wastes. The liquid wastes from a fruit and vegetable cannery pollute because they, like sewage, contain rich plant foods, including considerable sugar. If this liquid is run into silos that can be agitated and aerated, and in which the temperature can be controlled, and the liquid is made into an ideal nutrient culture by the addition of certain other plant foods, minerals, and trace elements, then inoculated with a mushroom culture, in an amazingly short while the potentially polluting materials can be turned into bountiful yields of mushroom mycelium.

Mycelium, the threadlike underground parts of the mushroom, has at least as much mushroom flavoring as the fruiting caps we ordinarily eat. The mycelium is removed from the liquid by centrifuging and resembles massive cakes of fresh yeast in appearance. There is an astonishing yield of nearly one pound of mycelium for each gallon of the culture medium, and because of the lower moisture content, each pound contains twice the weight of mushroom solids as does a pound of fresh mushrooms. This means that one pound of mycelium cake is equal to two pounds of fresh mushrooms in food value and flavoring ability.

Mycelium cake can be used in mushroom soups, gravies, and sauces, or anywhere that the texture of mushrooms is unimportant. The flavor concentration and quality can be improved by varying the culture medium, and this method of culture offers an ideal opportunity for breeding better and more highly flavored strains. A little of each batch is left to "seed" the next silo-ful of culture medium. The liquid that is centrifuged from the finished mycelium is nearly pure water and can be recycled through the cannery to pick up another load of nutrients.

A man at Scott Paper told me of experiments for using wastes from paper pulp-mills, among our worst polluters. A set-up much like the silos described above is inoculated with yeast. The paper industry could produce millions of tons of yeast from pulp-mill wastes if only there were a market for it. This yeast is not suitable for bakers, but is perfectly suitable for stock feed. Dried, it contains 37 percent protein and 39 percent carbohydrates, and it is loaded with vitamins that are hard to get from other sources.

Compounders of commercial livestock feeds already know the value of yeast, and include it in many mixed feeds. However, the amount they now use is severely limited, because if too much yeast is added to feed, the animals refuse to eat it. But there are thousands of species, strains, and varieties of yeast, so research could eventually produce a palatable yeast that would be one of the most economical feeds ever used. Already, there are ways around this problem of palatability.

When the processers of citrus fruits were finally forced to

clean up their wastes, they pressed the liquids from the wastes with powerful hydraulic presses, then dried the remaining pulp in a vacuum, leaving a dry citrus pulp that makes an excellent feed for dairy cattle. The juice first had several by-products removed from it, such as citrus oil and citric acid, then the remainder was concentrated to a citric molasses. This molasses is not palatable to human taste buds, but to cows it is ice cream and candy. They are so wild about it that they will eat feeds they ordinarily would not touch, if only a bit of citrus molasses is added. Let's get those citrus and paper people together and feed the cows some yeast à la mode.

What are we going to do with those old junk cars whose graveyards threaten to engulf the land with ugliness? In Hawaii they dissolve them in great vats of sulphuric acid to make iron sulphide, which makes pineapple-growing possible in soil that is very poor in available iron. But we have no use for as much iron sulphide as could be made with all the old cars one sees today. The junk-car problem was once solved, but we unsolved it. Formerly an old car was worth from $25 to $35 as scrap metal, which went back into new steel for more cars. Then the industry changed to a copper-bearing alloy that makes a better car but makes the metal unusable as scrap for reuse. The answer is obvious. Researchers must either come up with as good an alloy that does not destroy the metal's value for scrap, or the steelmaking methods must be altered to use the present alloy.

If any car, regardless of condition, could be made worth $25, then junkmen would come out of the woodwork to haul away all abandoned cars. Even if the steelmakers and automotive industry had to support this price artificially, it would be no more than right, and the extra cost would be passed on to the consumer, anyway. President Nixon has already proposed adding a $25 federal tax to automobiles to pay for disposing of them when they are worn out, but I'm very much afraid he is still thinking in terms of throwing them away, sinking them in the oceans, or burying them in landfill. Reuse of metals also preserves some very valuable natural resources. Metal ores are definitely finite, and I'd hate to think of my descendants having a shortage of these civilization-building materials.

The Stone Age, the Bronze Age, the Iron Age, the Atomic Age, and now the paper age. We live in a paper society. Each year 450 pounds of paper is discarded for each human being in our country, and most of it ends up in incinerators adding to air pollution. A great deal seems to be just kicked about as litter until it wears out. This is our greatest shame, for we already know perfectly well how to recycle paper to make more paper, but at present less than one percent of the waste paper is reused. Scrap paper not only can be used, but it makes very good paper for many purposes and it is economical. Newsprint and book stock can use a large percentage of waste paper in their pulp.

The place to start is with the consumer. Newspapers, magazines, and book publishers who publish articles supporting conservation and clean-up should be asked to put their actions where their words are, and use only such paper as contains at least a certain percentage of waste paper. The U.S. Government is the greatest single user of paper in the world. Let them demand that the paper they use contain waste paper. If this is done, the price of scrap paper will soar, and the awful paper litter that makes our cities and highways so unsightly will disappear. I foresee a day when a common household appliance will be a little paper baler, and local Boy Scout and Girl Scout troops and other worthwhile organizations will keep their treasuries solvent by collecting and selling this paper. They will feel good about it in another way, too. Each ton of waste paper that is recycled saves 17 trees from being cut down.

I call on the youth of America to get those brilliant young minds to work on creative ideas for solving our pollution problems. These problems will finally be solved, not by demonstrations, fights, or name-calling. They will be solved by human ingenuity, applied with love, for love is a powerful form of pressure which few are prepared to resist. The solution of our ecological problems starts in your heart.

Index

Index